The Ghosts of St. Ann's Past
Stories of St. Ann's Orphanage Worcester, Mass.

Joseph Massie
&
Rosalie Massie Blackburn

This book is dedicated to all the orphans, boarders, their families, the Grey Nuns (Sisters of Charity) of Montreal and all the people who have been a part of St. Ann's French Canadian Orphanage since its inception in 1889.

Table of Contents

Acknowledgement

This book would not have been possible without the help and inspiration of all the people who have had their lives affected by St. Ann's French Canadian Orphanage in Worcester, Mass. The photos, memories and stories they shared has helped us create a fact based story that spans more than seventy-five years.

Much appreciation to the Archives of the Grey Nuns of Montreal (Sisters of Charity) for allowing us access to the St. Ann's French Canadian Orphanage Worcester, Mass. historical documents and photo albums they have in their facility.

The internet proved to be the greatest tool of all in our search into the background of St. Ann's Orphanage in Worcester, Mass. It guided us to websites where past residents, families and friends also searched for information. They left blogs for us and others to see. That led us to locations that provided us with photos, maps, newspaper clippings, and articles from St. Ann's past.

In archived, local area newspapers we were able to find an assortment of historical and interesting articles. They include the Catholic Free Press, the Worcester Telegram, the Worcester Gazette and the Boston Globe.

We are grateful for our St. Ann's Orphanage Worcester, Mass. Facebook page which provides many of our followers a look back into our history through the use of shared photos and stories. Our photo albums grow larger with each passing day.

Chapter 1

A Road Trip of a Life Time

ST. ANN'S FRENCH CANADIAN ORPHANAGE

In the wee hours of April 16th I was briskly shaken awake by my wife, Christine. Usually it was due to my heavy, rhythmic breathing or intrusive snoring, but this night was different. She told me I kept yelling out, "Bernadette, please don't go! I still have so many questions to ask you!" It was apparent we were not going to fall back to sleep any time soon.

We headed to our kitchen dinette area and were greeted by my sister Rosie who was visiting us from Florida. Wiping the sleep from her eyes she inquired. "What in the world was all that screaming and who is Bernadette?" So, we sat down to a hot cup of tea as I began recalling my dream.

"The day started like any other. We were sitting around this same table reminiscing about the memories we each had of St. Anne's Orphanage. It was finally decided that we would take a road trip to Worcester, Massachusetts to visit our childhood home, a place we have not been to for more than sixty years. Little did we know this trip was about to change our lives forever. Off we went on a seventy-mile drive to visit the source of all our questions, St. Anne's Orphanage."

As we approached 133 Granite Street we saw the remnants of some worn torn buildings. There was a failing fence that once protected a swimming pool. It was now delegated to surrounding a worn torn parking lot. As we pulled alongside the fence we saw a single story complex and some apartment like buildings flowing down the hill behind it. Obviously, we were seeing the dilapidated buildings of Mount St. Ann that had replaced the original St. Anne's Orphanage buildings in 1970.

Across the street from the fenced lot was the Grotto of Our Lady of Lourdes, once reputed to be one of the most beautiful of shrines in New England. We vividly remembered praying there alongside many residents of St. Ann's Orphanage. This once beautiful grotto now looked so gray and dismal.

A black wrought iron fence enslaved this sacred site. The arched curves of the stone structure were still there but the ivy that once grew along the stone facing no longer blanketed the structure. You could see Saint Bernadette still kneeling in prayer facing the Holy Mother of Jesus.

With great trepidation we crossed Granite Street to the gated grotto. I attempted to open the gates only to be hampered by the rust encrusted hinges. It finally took two of us to loosen its grip. The squealing pierced our ears as we swung open the double gated entry. We slowly trudged up the stone slabs that we once were able to prance up so easily in our youth. As we approached the top steps we could see the Virgin Mary, just as beautiful as we remembered, tucked into her nook within the stone masonry.

We walked past the statue of Saint Bernadette and turned to face her. There she was kneeling with her hands crossed over her heart. We were horrified to see that her face had been battered about the mouth and nose. Her eyes still looking up toward Mary.

It reminded us that Bernadette had suffered so much during her short life. She had been sickly throughout her life and was condemned for her visons of Mary. She gave up her chance of being healed by the sacred spring she had found allowing others to be cured by the pure waters the spring brought forth.

"Bonjour mes amis. Je suis tellement reconnaissante d'avoir quelqu'un visite."

Our hearts nearly leapt into our throats as we witnessed this statuette kneeling in front of us come to life. We were so startled we could barely speak. Rosalie blurted out, "Forgive us but we no longer speak French." "Mais Oui. I understand." Said Bernadette, "I am so grateful to have you visit. I am but a humble servant to the mother of Jesus, the Blessed Virgin Mary. When I was a young girl I was granted audience to her on eighteen separate occasions. I pray here as I did those many years ago."

As we came to our senses we began to converse with Saint Bernadette. "Why would you present yourself to us, or anybody, after being here for so long?" I asked. "Well, monsieur, the time has come that this home for thousands of our Lord's children will no longer be with us. Soon the last of St. Ann's French Canadian Orphanage and Mount St. Ann will be demolished, never to serve abandoned or needy children again.

"Joe, Rosie! Look, over there." Said Christine. "Everything has changed! We are no longer here, I mean, in 2015! What's going on?" "Oh my God!" blurted Rosalie, "You're right!" Across the street no longer stood the worn out buildings of Mount St. Ann but the buildings we remembered so vividly from our youth. A rush of pure astonishment came over us.

"Do not be alarmed mes amis." said Bernadette with a calming voice. "You have come here to visit your past at a time when there will be no future. So we have decided that you three will be our voice to all those families and friends who have been a part of this wondrous place. Your quest is meant to bring some answers and to enlighten those who seek the foundation of their existence."

"How can we do this?" I asked. "There is nothing special about us. We are just regular people looking for answers to our past. We were only at St. Ann's Orphanage for a couple years. All we remember are faded memories and dreams. Some of them have just recently been brought back to us by our new findings."

Saint Bernadette's reply was gracious and thoughtful. "You took the time and effort to research your past. You did this unselfish act for all the members of the St. Ann's family, not just for yourselves. You made our choice an easy one. So, come. I will start you on a journey that will further inspire you to pass on to others the how and why St. Ann's French Canadian Orphanage has affected thousands of people. This will be a journey you will not soon forget."

I reached out my hand to assist Bernadette in rising from the spot she had knelt for so many years. Her tiny hand felt cool and soft. A rush of calm and serenity fell over me. I reached out to touch Christine who in turn took hold of Rosalie. The same calmness and serenity invaded their bodies. Like endeared servants we followed Saint Bernadette as she guided us out of the now beautiful, gateless grotto across Granite Street to the four story wooden structure that stood there for over seventy-five years. We were indeed on our way to an adventure of biblical proportions!

Chapter 2

As it was in the Beginning

HOW IT ALL GOT STARTED

We entered the building midway along the Granite Street side. Here was the building where we had attended our first years of schooling. The halls were dark and the wood planks of the hallways creaked as we walked along, side-by-side, hand-in-hand. We followed Bernadette as she turned into a dark room. Its features were hard to make out. It looked like a sitting room from an old Victorian house. "Please, mes amis, sit." begged Bernadette. "I am about to leave you with those whose lives were touched by St. Ann's French Canadian Orphanage."

Christine broke in with an obvious question. "I'm sorry, but do you mean we will be visited by ghosts of St. Ann's past? Kind of like the apparitions in the Dickens' novel about Scrooge?" "Mais oui." smiled Bernadette. "But not so dramatic. This is about reality not fiction." She continued in a solemn voice, "Just as I had encountered eighteen visions of our Virgin Mary, you three will encounter eighteen visions of St. Ann's past. Some will guide you through the moments and memories of their time here. Some will be the embodiment of thoughts or dreams blossoming forth from the minds and spirits of children and adults alike. Cherish each one and remember their stories. I shall return in good time. I bid you adieu." Saint Bernadette turned away and faded into the shadows of the dark room.

We all looked at each other in astonishment as our eyes were better focused to the darkness. The place we were in did not bring back any memories from our time at St. Ann's. We decided to look about the premises in search of an answer. As we passed through the doorway we entered a large foyer with a large staircase on one side and a large door leading to the outside. The thought did enter our minds to head quickly for the door. "Look." said Christine as she pointed to the top of the stairs. "Do you guys see what I see?"

Perched at the top of the staircase was a gray feminine figure. Her long flowing garment had what looked like a black hoodie draped over her shoulders and head. At heart level was a crucifix that sparkled even in the dim light. Her eyes peered at us through goggle like glasses. The stairs made an eerie creaking sound as she slowly descended. She spoke with a strong Canadian accent. "Bonsoir mes amis, je suis Victoria. Ah, pardonnez-moi. I am sorry. English is not my first language. I am Sister Victoria. Our beloved Bernadette has informed me of your arrival. Monsieur Joseph, and Madame Rosalie and Christine I welcome you to the beginning of my life's journey. I was one of the first children to enter this boarding home."

Bonsoir Sister Victoria." I replied. "Then this must be the old house on Southgate Street in Worcester. I read accounts that this was not a safe or happy place to live." Sister Victoria passed off my comment and began to explain her reason for meeting with them. "First, I will provide you with the details of how this establishment came to be. Then, I will present you with a fantasy like tour of my home at the 'Farm'."

"It was during my stay at the farm when I became aware of my calling to the Lord and desire to become a Grey Nun. Come into the sitting room so I may provide you with a bit of history." We did as she instructed and settled into the provided settees and armchairs neatly placed about the room. Sister Victoria began her lecture on the orphanage's beginning. It wasn't quite the school day memories we had as children but we did make those comparisons.

"Many people believe St. Ann's Orphanage was started by the Sisters of Charity, better known as the Grey Nuns of Montreal. But the Grey Nuns didn't come into the picture until 1891. Its roots actually started in 1889, the year I was placed into this orphans' home with my three sisters. My mother became deathly ill when I was eight years old. We were part of the first group of children to live here."

SISTER VICTORIA BESSETTE, S.G.M., VISITS ST
Grey Nun, 65, returns to school she attended

"You see," continued Sister Victoria, "It all started when Father Joseph Brouillet, the pastor of Notre Dame des Canadiens Parish in Worcester, wanted to build a school and orphanage for orphaned children and the elderly. He was concerned about the plight of the children left parentless and the elderly left to fend for themselves. In those poverty stricken times they would not have survived without help."

"He also wanted to start up a religious order to teach and care for those unfortunate people living in Worcester's fast growing Franco-American community. He worked with Father Alexis Delphos, the pastor of St. Denis Parish in East Douglas, of which St. Anne's church was a mission. Father Delphos granted permission to two teachers at St. Anne's Parish to take simple religious vows and wear the habit of the Third Order of St. Francis."

"Father Brouillet rented a three story house on Southgate Street. This two story annex we are sitting in was quickly built as new residents, both young and old, quickly filled the house. My memory evades me, but I believe this orphanage was originally called The French-Canadian Orphanage of Worcester. Father Brouillet recruited and trained new members of the order over the next year. Eight novices were quickly brought in to help." "Novices?" interrupted Rosalie. "Oui, replied Sister Victoria. "These are young ladies who are received into the order for a probation period before taking their vows."

Sister Victoria continued her thought process. "They had to care for the children and elderly all the while cleaning, cooking, mending clothes and keeping the building in good repair. Every day, two of them went out into the community to beg for money, food, clothing and other supplies. It was their only source of income. They received support from the Franco-American community, from many in the city's large Irish community and even from some in the Protestant community. The new annex and the growing number of orphans, stretched their funds very thin."

"Things started out as expected. Unfortunately, it didn't last for long." Sister Victoria gave a little smirk. "I guess you could say Father Brouillet became a bit too ambitious. He asked the sisters to expand their ministry to an orphanage in Fall River and to an old farm in Auburn. There were only 14 novices to work all three places and it proved too much. OK, without dragging out the story, here's the short version."

"There were disagreements and misunderstandings between the sisters and Father Brouillet. The sisters wanted to incorporate the Third Order of St. Francis and thought it had been approved. But Bishop Patrick O'Reilly told them the founding of a new religious community in the Springfield Diocese had not been authorized. Of course, the founding ladies were not very happy. So they packed up and went off to Canada."

"Eventually a solution was worked out. Their disagreements with Father Brouillet was put aside. They returned from Canada with their order now reestablished as the Little Franciscans of Mary. Because their Mother House was in Canada Bishop O'Reilly accepted them into the Springfield Diocese as missionaries. There was one condition. They had to take charge of the elderly that were at the orphanage. The orphans would become the full time responsibility of the Grey Nuns."

"Now I can see how the Grey Nuns fit into this soap opera." Said Christine. "But please, continue." Christine was right. We were all listening intently to this story with its twists and turns. We had not been expecting such drama in what was thought to be a straight forward story.

"So, as you can see, elaborated Sister Victoria. "A lot happened during those first two years." We all resettled ourselves

14

in our seats as she continued. "The Orphan Home started out as a haven for all those in need, young and old. With the disagreements and the situation seemingly getting out of hand a split up was eminent. Father Brouillet turned to the Grey Nuns of Montreal. On January 31, 1891 The Sisters of Charity sent Sister Anna Piche and others to manage the orphan home. They too found the difficulty of caring for the residents without means and had to find ways to procure funds."

"1891 was a new beginning for two new establishments. The order of the Little Franciscans of Mary took charge of the elderly as they had agreed and moved to a different facility. The order of the Grey Nuns remained to care for the orphaned children. The Grey Nuns soon purchased a large farm with over 149 sprawling acres on Granite Street. There was a large farm house, a barn and stable at the top of the hill." Victoria paused and looked upward. "I dearly remember that farm. So many dear memories."

She continued her history lesson. "Not that I remembered at that time, but the Society of Benefactors was organized that year. They provided us with $15,000 so that a new building to shelter us could be built. I surely remember the excitement we all felt. We were going to move into a wonderful new home. There would be lots of space to run around," she paused. "and farm animals." Again, we could see the gleam in Sister Victoria's eyes as her face glowed with excitement.

"They began building this big white four-story wooden structure. I was later told it was typical to the style of other institutions of that period. It contained a school, dormitories, a chapel, and the needed kitchen and bath amenities. It could house nearly 200 children. Preparation was underway for our move. Our numbers were quickly increasing so ten more Grey Nun missionaries were sent to help support us."

"Well, in the year of our Lord 1892, on the 27th of February, an Agreement of Association was signed and notarized and the St. Ann's French Canadian Orphanage was incorporated. So, you see, it took about two years to get the orphans home properly established and St. Ann's French Canadian Orphanage became official. Over the years the spelling of the name Ann would be interchanged with Anne. At one point a determined sister tried to change the official document by placing the letter e upon it. It is readily seen as an illegal insert. Even though Anne is commonly used, Ann would always be the official spelling."

"On January 3, 1893 Mother Superior Anna Piche, along with the other Grey Nuns and all of us children moved into our new home. Fourteen acres of the massive site were utilized for farming. We were still very poor and everyone worked the farm, tended the animals, took care of the massive home and made clothes to make ends meet. Everyone had chores to do inside and out. We grew vegetables, and made a lot of our own food from the crops and animals. New orphans were continually welcomed into our home."

Again, we saw her pause as her memories cascaded about her thoughts. Sister Victoria rose and walked to the large window. "Instead of me prattling on, see for yourselves. Please, come to the window and gaze upon the sights below. A fantasy filled story is unfolding about the time we moved into our new home high on the hills of Granite Street." We rushed to the window where a whole new wonderment filled our eyes and ears. It was as if we were watching a 3-D movie.

DOWN ON THE FARM

To our amazement we were gazing down at a scene unfolding in a barn. It was almost as if we were floating above, looking down from the loft. Animals were gathering to the open area of the barn where a pair of horses stood. They seemed to be in charge of the group. Just below us we saw the images or an old man and woman. They seemed to be maneuvering behind a pile of hay stacked high in the corner of the barn.

"Oh what a beautiful day." thought Rosanna. The barnyard was ablaze with chatter. There was Ernest, her beloved husband of 65 years, heading toward her. They were interested in seeing why the animals had all gathered together. They appeared to be conversing about something. "Hey Rosy, what's going on with the animals?" "I'm not sure Ernest, but it seems something has gotten them all a flutter. If we stay silent and listen, we may be able to understand their muddling." Ernest and Rosanna ducked behind the hay stack. "They may have heard about the farm being sold. We will soon have new owners here along with some orphaned children. I'm sure these children will need lots of care and love."

"Yes, replied Ernest. "A group called the Grey Nuns bought Ellsworth Farm and will build an orphan home here. I can't believe they bought the entire 150 acres. I can understand them buying the 100 acres on this side of Granite Street but they also purchased the western 50 acres across the street. Well, they must really be serious about this farm, Eh?" "Rosanna responded, "My guess is our farm will come alive again. It's been too long since children played in these fields." A smile of happy days long past came over their faces.

"I'm sure the Grey Nuns and children will do their parts to care for the animals and all the gardens. It will be hard work but the fruit of their labor will make them prosper and strong." "Oh Ernest, it will be so wonderful to have children here again, there is nothing better than a child's laughter." "Yes, my dear Rosy, and maybe this is what has gotten these animals so riled up." "Shush, said Rosanna, it sounds like they're settling down."

In the midst of this multitude of farm animals towered a jet black horse. It stood like a monument over the rest of the group. Its shoulders and withers were so muscular. It was plain to see this horse had done its fair share of plowing and other farm work. With its head raised high he demanded notice. "Okay my friends, please quiet down. We don't want to attract attention here." said Charlie in a calming bray. "Whyyyy?" bleated a goat in the back of the crowd. "It's not as if anyone understands what we're saying." Charlie ignored the goat and continued on. "We all know that the farm has been sold but to whom we are not sure!"

18

Artwork by Soher Jesus Silva-Alvarado

"Please Charlie, what will happen to us?" said Homer the hog. "Will we stay here or be sold? Or, or, we could be sentenced to…. Ahhh, I feel dizzy. I think I'm going to faint!" "Oh my," said Lola the cat. "I can't die. Who will help keep the rats and pests in control? Hoot needs my help to scout out and remove those varmints." "HOOT HOOT!" said the owl. "We are all useful here. Our purpose is to keep this farm safe and productive." "Amen to that." barked Joker the big German Shepard. "If I am not here who will guard the farm from unwanted people, like poachers and thieves? There are other large preying animals out there that could attack any one of you."

"Alright," clucked Mrs. Murphy, the mother hen from the house of chickens. "Listen up. I heard it straight from the horse's mouth. That's Old Clive, not you Charlie." She cackled. All the animals laughed in their own peculiar ways. "He heard a group of humans talking at the farm house when he was tied up to the front rail. It appears we are about to receive a gaggle of children and some adults they were calling Grey Nuns. We all know what children are and how wonderful they can be. They know how to share their love and laughter."

"It's pure Joy!" neighed Winnie the mare, Charlies' wife. "But what are these creatures they call Grey Nuns?" Lola purred. "I can't wait to get hugged and scratched behind my ears by the children." "Baaaa," bleated Betty the ewe. "No one knows what's going to happen but we will soon find out. I hope they will be friendly to us?" "Well," mooed Frederica the cow, "seems to me these Grey Nuns are coming to care for the children so they can't be that bad. Children can't take care of themselves!"

"Okay, said Charlie. "We all need to calm down. It seems like we are getting a good family for the farm. Let's wait and see what happens. I believe our new family will stay here for a long time. We must do our very best to give them joy and to help the children and these Grey Nuns. Now let's get back to doing what we do best, making this farm a happy and productive place to live." The herd of animals slowly headed towards their own parts of the barn and stable.

"It looks like the animals have calmed down." whispered Rosanna to Ernest. "I bet they are worried about what might happen to them once the Grey Nuns come and take over the farm." "They need not worry their little hooves." replied Ernest in a quiet voice. "Maybe I should go and talk to them Ernest. I think they would understand me. Eh?" "Of course they will Rosy. Besides being a kind and loving person, your voice will give them the comfort they need right now. And don't forget, we are no longer of this earth and can easily converse with all our animal friends." "Oh yes, said Rosanna. "I keep forgetting that."

20

Ernest left the barn so that Rosanna could explain the situation to the farm animals. The young pups, Gracie and Gunner had no interest in all the politics and followed Ernest out the barn. They spotted Rocky the squirrel and a good chase around the barn yard was afoot.

ST. ANN'S FRENCH CANADIAN ORPAHANGE

The three of us turned to one another to converse. "Jeepers!" said Rosalie, "This whole thing is amazing. Here we are somewhere in time, sitting somewhere I don't know and watching animals and ghosts talk to each other." Sister Victoria smiled. "The Lord does work in mysterious ways." "You bet," I said. "This is awesome!" "It's better than sticking those 3-D glasses on your face." Said Christine. "Shhh, retorted Rosalie, "I hear something going on out there." They all turned their attention back toward the window.

"Look at that." Said Christine. "What a majestic looking building. It seems to have just popped up from nowhere." Rosalie chuckled. "Toto, I don't think we're in Kansas anymore." She looked at me and Christine and giggled. "You know I just had to say that." We all laughed then returned our gazes back toward the sights unfolding before us.

A white, four story building was positioned alongside Granite Street. Just to the south was a barn and stable. A little further south was a pair of two story farm houses with chimneys extending skyward on both ends of the houses. To the north and east of these structures was a beautiful view of the falling hillside and the Worcester landscape off in the distance.

From our perch we could see carriages and buckboards queued up along Granite Street. Men were unloading the transports laden with furniture and household goods. A large group of children were marching two-by-two up Granite Street toward the farm. They looked weary from their hour long trek from Southgate Street. The older children seemed to be chaperoning the younger ones. A few Grey Nuns were overlooking the maneuvers.

As the children approached their new home we could see them getting excited. They bobbed their heads all about not knowing where to look first. They were in awe of the large white building coming into their view. They whispered to each other and pointed toward the landscapes on both sides of the road. Eventually they became fixated at what they saw lounging about the barnyard.

The longtime residents of the farm were about to meet their new family. "Can we go see them?" cried 11-year-old Vickie as she pointed toward the mixed herd of animals. Mother Superior nodded approval as she commanded them. "Remember, these animals aren't house pets. Don't scare them. Be kind to them and they will be kind to you." Without hesitation, the children dashed off toward the barn with Sister Marie and the chaperones in tow.

"Okay everyone. Listen up." commanded Charlie. "Here come the children. They all look so excited running toward us. Remember, don't scare them. Be kind to them and they will be kind to you." He turned to Whinny. "It's like they've never seen farm animals before." Excitement and wonder filled Winnie's eyes. "I believe we are going to enjoy their company."

Out of nowhere came Gunner and Gracie. They dashed to the children with so much excitement. Love and joy filled the children's hearts as the puppies jumped and licked as many of the kids they could get to. "Oh how wonderful it is to have so many little humans for pets. We will surely take good care of them."

"Oh no!" barked Joker. "What is that creature following them? I've never seen anything like that before. Let me go sniff it out." Sniff, sniff. Slowly a human hand reached out from the folds of the garment and slowly moved toward Joker. Sniff, sniff. "Well, it smells human to me. I'd say a bit odd looking though."

To most, the Grey Nuns would appear a bit odd. They were dressed in thick heavy gray gowns and had gray and black hooded things covering their heads. They also spoke a weird language. "Regardez ces beaux animaux et quel beau chien." ("Look at these beautiful animals and what a wonderful dog.")

"All I can see are two eyes, a nose and mouth." snorted Homer the hog. Billy bleated out. "They have no hair or ears. Maaaybe they're aliens from outer space or something." "I know what they are." hooted Hoot in a wise manner. "They are a new breed of human. Yep that's it." "Well they seem to be nice." Purred Lola. "This one is scratching behind my ear! Oh my! That's it. Right there. Purrrrrr."

The group of children made their way to the animals petting them and talking in their strange language. As the children approached the chickens Mother Hen Murphy started cackling. "No human or any other animal is going to touch me. I'll peck their eyes out before I let them manhandle me." All the other hens in the barn yard started cackling and running about. "Let's go ladies. This is no place for us. Back to our roosts."

A yell came from Mother Superior calling the children back to the house. "It is time for our afternoon prayers before we prepare for the evening meal. You must get in your groups and properly line up for washing hands and faces." The children quickly obeyed her command and headed toward the house.

Francis decided to delay his return by continuing his encounter with the animals. Sister Marie noticed his indolence and swoosh, her hand appeared from her garment and instantly put a vise like grip on his ear. "When Mother Superior commands you, you never hesitate. Do you understand Master Francois?" "Yes, Sister Marie." Whined Francis as he tried to loosen her grip. "Well, it looks like you will be doing extra kitchen work tonight. Now move it before I fetch my ruler!" Francis winched in pain as he ran up to the group and returned to his rightful place in line.

SPARE THE ROD AND SPOIL THE CHILD

Rosalie turned away from the window. "They used the ruler even back then?" "Of course they did." I said. "Most people don't know that many forms of corporal punishment have been used for centuries. All the way to the late 1900's children were brutalized with rulers, canes, sticks, switches, leather straps, and even the books they studied. Both mental and physical abuse were very common back then. Believe it or not, it was used everywhere. I mean in schools, all kinds of institutions, including St. Ann's, and even in the privacy of ones' home. This atrocity wasn't legally stopped until about 50 years ago."

"That's right." Said Christine. "I remember kids in my school being smacked across the knuckles and even their backsides with a ruler or stick. When kids in the classroom couldn't answer the teacher's questions they were stood in the corner of the room. Some were even made to wear a dunce cap."

"Yah, said Rosalie. "I remember those things too." I chuckled. "Huh, I remember my first grade teacher made a boy get under her long heavy dress right in front of the whole class because he was flipping girls' dresses up while at recess in the school yard." "I remember you telling me that a long time ago." said Rosalie. "Kids don't know how good they have it nowadays."

We turned to Sister Victoria for some words of encouragement. Her report only confirmed these happenings. "As a child I was not subjected to harsh punishment as I was heartfelt to please my Lord. I would get the occasional wrap on the knuckles for my failure to control one of my charges. It made me stronger and more focused at my duties. Others were not so fortunate. They would receive whatever punishment deemed appropriate for the situation."

"Yes, discipline was seen as a necessity tool to control the children. If you could not control one, then you could not control any." Sister Victoria sighed. "A lot of us did not condone some methods of punishment. But at the time these types of punishments were the norm. Over time more sisters stood up to the unnecessary abuse and eventually it was removed from the institutions. Praise the Lord."

"You know," I said. "all you hear about is the abuse or punishment being handed out. How about how hard it was for the orphanage to survive day to day? Stop and think about what had to be done to take care of some 200 children. Clothing had to be made fixed or purchased. Making three meals a day for all these children. The staff had to figure out where the food was coming from. You can't get food out of the garden in the dead of winter. Just think how many chickens or pigs it would take to feed the children each day. You still had to find a way to buy porridge or cereal. You may be living on a farm but, have you ever seen a rich farmer? From the day St. Ann's Orphanage began until the day it closed living in poverty was all they knew."

"You are so right, Joseph." replied Sister Victoria. "Some years were better than others. When the summer provided us with a good crop we were able to can and store more for the winter months. The basic needs, like bread, were more difficult to get. When it seemed all hope was lost our prayers would be answered. To many people St. Ann's French Canadian Orphanage was nothing but a name. But to others it was a place where they could give of their time, energy and money as a means of doing unto others what they wish to be done to themselves. Every day I thank the Lord and the people of Worcester, Massachusetts for their support."

THE CHAPEL OF ST. ANN'S ORPHANAGE

We started to hear stomping of feet and loud murmurs coming from the window. We maneuvered ourselves closer to the window's opening to get a better view. Sister Victoria nestled close to us so she too could get a good look at the proceedings. I guess she was looking for young Vickie and her sisters. We saw the children mustering into a beautiful chapel. The girls filed into the pews on the left and the boys to the right. The youngest toward the front.

As we looked around we remembered the layout from the many hours we spent in this chapel when we were children. The statues of Mary to the left and Joseph to the right of the altar were still there. We could see this chapel was brand new. Many other statues adorned the front and sides of the chapel. The altar looked like a castle tower rising to the heavens. There were dormers to each side of the tower and candelabras dawned the altar.

At the front of the gathering stood Father Joseph Brouillet alongside Father Zotique Durocher, who was the first chaplain of St. Ann's French Canadian Orphanage. Father Durocher led the afternoon prayers while the nuns walked the aisles to insure the children were attentive. After the prayer session, Bishop Patrick T. O'Reilly who had come all the way from Springfield, Massachusetts gave the Benediction. He blessed the children and their new home. His final words, "Dominus vobiscum," were followed by the children's unison voices, "Et cum spiritu tuo."

("The Lord be with you." "And with your spirit.") He stepped down from the altar and departed the proceedings through the vestibule.

Mother Superior took over the proceedings. "Today is a new beginning for all of us. We have been blessed with this farm and new home and must repay the Lord and all others who have provided for us. It will be a long and arduous journey. We must all obey the rules and complete our daily chores without question. We are now farmers and must think and act as a farmer's family. The animals and the crops are a vital part of our livelihood. If they are not properly cared for we will all suffer the consequences. There will be no excuses. You must now listen to what your daily routines and duties are from this day forward."

A gesture to one of her novices resulted in a chalk board being moved into position in front of the altar. It neatly displayed a chart of her plan. "The day will start bright and early with the sisters and the older girls and boys rising for the new day. While the sisters prepare breakfast, these girls and boys will quickly wash, dress and make their beds. They will gather in the dining room to eat breakfast."

"Afterwards, they will move on to their daily routines. The older girls and boys who have charges will proceed to the dormitories and roust up the youngsters from their sleep. The young charges will follow directions without haste. If there are any issues the dormitory sister will confront and correct them."

As the Mother Superior walked up the aisle she pointed toward the blackboard. "The older girls without charges will check the duty roster to find out where their daily duties will be performed. The duty roster will be posted in the dormitories and in the hall just inside the main entrance. You may be part of the kitchen help, or assisting in our newly equipped sewing rooms. You may find yourself in the basement tending to the irons and helping with the laundry and ironing."

"The chickens will need feeding and the eggs collected. Other chores will be assigned as needed. Once the older girls have readied their charges they too will check the duty roster for their assignments. These girls must insure the youngsters are taught how to do their chores. Remember, the morning chores must be completed by the time the school sessions begin."

She turned toward the boys and with a stern voice said, "The boys' roster will be posted alongside the girls' roster. The boys who have charges will follow the same routine as the girls while the other boys will check their listed duties. Gentlemen, most of you will be tending the farm. So that no one feels they are working harder than the other, you will find yourselves rotating chores."

"You may be plowing and planting the fields, or weeding and grooming the gardens. There are animals to be fed and groomed and hogs to be slopped. You might be assigned to gather, cut and split wood for the fires. Household chores are also possible during bad weather. A farm has many chores that must be completed in a timely manner."

As Mother Superior returned to the altar she turned and made one final statement. "We must all do our duty to ourselves and to the Lord. Obey not and you will feel the hand of the Lord upon you. Do as you are told without question or complaint and we all shall be rewarded with His blessings and grace. Are there any questions?" Without a pause she continued, "Do you all understand?" A loud, "Yes, Mother Superior," echoed around the chapel.

The window scene faded to dark as the children rose and began to exit the chapel. We settled back into our seats and looked at each other. It was at that moment we realized Sister Victoria was no longer with us. "I guess Sister Victoria has moved on," said Christine. I replied. "I guess the story she wanted to convey to us is complete. So far we have seen how the orphanage got started and how they began their lives on the farm."

"Well then," said Rosalie. "What happens now?" Christine pointed to the doorway and said, "We met up with Sister Victoria after walking through that doorway. Maybe that is the way to our next encounter." We all stood up and walked toward the doorway with great anticipation.

Chapter 3

A Fair of the Heart

THE NEW MILLENNIUM

We passed into the foyer where we previously met up with Sister Victoria but found no one to greet us. We glanced up the stairway and down the hallways but saw nothing. We only heard the noises of an old creaking building. "Christine said. "I guess there's nothing left for us to see in this place. Maybe it's time we left." We turned and walked toward the exit. As we approached the doorway we could hear what sounded like horse hooves clip clopping outside. As the doors swung open we were greeted to a bright light and our next encounter.

"Bonjour, mes amis." called out a young man who was standing next to a double seated buckboard filled in the back with an array of vegetables. It appeared that we had stepped into the scene outside the four story orphanage building we had just viewed from the sitting room window. In the front seat of the buckboard was a young teenaged looking boy and in the back seat sat a much younger girl. "Come my friends we have so much to do today. We must get this produce to the fair before the hot sun starts to spoil it." "Bon jour." I replied. What should we call you?" Oh, pardonnez-moi. My name is Robert. I am one of the work hands here on the farm."

"Please, let me assist you beautiful ladies." Robert took hold of Rosalie and Christine and assisted them into the rear seat. The young girl was seated between them. "Hello sweetie," said Rosalie. "My name is Rosalie and this is Christine. You may call us Rosie and Chrissy if you'd like. What is your name?" "Bonjour, my name is Violette. That is Otto sitting in the front seat. That's where the boys sit."

Robert instructed me to be seated in the front on the other side of Otto. As I climbed into the buckboard I noticed the original orphanage building had an addition to it on the north side. Robert noticed my glance and spoke before I had a chance. "Yes, my friend. We are passing though time not too long after this wonderful addition was gifted to us by Mrs. Georgiette Bowman Wood."

"She was the daughter of the Mr. George Crompton whose family brought prosperity to the Worcester area with the latest innovations and inventions for the manufacturing industry." There was a slight pause before he continued. "A sad story did befall her. You see, her husband Albert, she had been married to for less than two years, passed away at the young age of 31."

"She had been very pleased with the orphanage and all that was accomplished here. It was to St. Ann's French Canadian Orphanage that she gifted her beautiful house you see before you. Rosalie interjected. "This is the same place we came to know when we were young. Have you been in there Violette?" "No madam Rosie. That is where the sisters and Mother Superior live and pray. Only special older girls are allowed in there so they can see to the daily needs of the nuns."

With Robert's flick of the reins the two strong horses jerked forward and pulled our wagon northbound along Granite Street. Otto began his rendition of how the new addition came to be placed here. "What a day it was when this grand house was added to ours. The horses were struggling to pull this monstrous house that was set upon so many axels and wheels. No traffic could move along Granite Street for most of the day. All of the children and nuns stood in awe as they watched a group of men maneuver it slowly onto the foundation that had just been built for the occasion."

"It is now used strictly by the nuns. They have their own bedrooms, and eating area. They will soon have one of the larger rooms converted into a small chapel. The other large sitting room is where the Sister Superior and her assistants meet with people dropping off children into their care. It is also the exit way for those kids lucky enough to be adopted or going back home to family."

Before we knew it we were seeing people mulling about in their yards and moving through the streets. It was easy going as we made our way down Vernon Street and onto Green. Christine asked, "Robert, you mentioned we are going to a fair." Robert remarked. "Yes, that is so. Each year, on the first weekend of

September, there is the Great Worcester Fair where the public can go to see marvelous things and for the locals to show and sell their goods. These fairs have been a God send for the orphanage in so many ways."

"What about you, Robert." I asked. "You appear to be in your twenties. So how do you fit in with St. Ann's French Canadian Orphanage?" Robert's reply was interesting to say the least. "It seems people forget about the help when they speak of things in their past. As I mentioned earlier, I am one of the hired farm hands. My Memere and Pepere were also farm hands long ago." Christine interjected. "You are referring to the older couple we saw earlier? Rosanna and Ernest?"

"Yes, madam Chrissy. They were my grandparents. It was only fit that I had the opportunity to work the same farm they did so long ago. Pepere was so fond of his flower garden. St. Ann's has rejuvenated it and children like Otto have come to love working in it. A Sunday service does not start until the flowers from the garden are adorned throughout the chapel."

We turned left onto Park Street heading for Main when Robert pointed out a church to our right. "There is Notre Dame des Canadiens. That is where the idea of our orphanage was conceived by Father Brouillet." We were without a doubt in the heart of the city. We passed a park on the right with a large building adjacent to it just before we turned right onto Main Street.

Otto spoke out with undo excitement. "I remember this place! This is City Hall. We came here to see the President of the United States." "Is this so?" asked Rosalie. "We most certainly did!" said Robert. "Do you children remember his name?" Violette and Otto responded in unison. "President William H. Taft." "Very well done." replied Robert. "I see you two remembered your history lessons." "Jeepers." replied Rosalie as she gave Violette a little hug. "You guys are pretty lucky seeing the president."

"Yes, my friends, we were also fortunate enough to get a great location along Main Street right here in front of City Hall. It was Sunday, April 3, 1910 when the president visited Worcester, His motorcar passed right by our group of orphans. He even had the driver slow down so the children could get a good look at him. His smiles and hand waves made a big impression on them."

President Taft and Governor Draper passing Worcester City Hall, April 3, 1910, en route for Train Service Men's Convention at Mechanic Hall

"I can imagine." said Christine. "It must have been a once in a lifetime thing to see the president back in those days." "When we grew up we were able to see all the presidents on television." Both Otto and Violette turned toward Christine with an odd expression on their faces. "Sorry, I forgot where and when we are."

Robert pulled the reins ever so slightly and the horses heeded his command turning left onto Elm Street. "I have taken the liberty of bringing you past the old Agricultural Grounds that was set across the street from Elm Park. That is where the Great Worcester Fair was held for so many years. It was a good place for the fair and a bit closer for us to travel. But, times have changed and we now must travel to Indian Lake in the Greendale section of Worcester where the new fair is being held. It is much grander and is called the New England Fair."

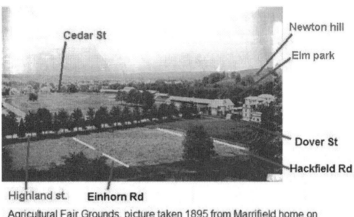

Agricultural Fair Grounds, picture taken 1895 from Marrifield home on Shussler Rd
send corrections to jim28518@yahoo.com

At the end of Elm Street, we turned right onto Park Ave. As we traversed Newton Hill we gazed down upon the grand view of Elm Park. On the other side of the park we could see the remnants of the old fairgrounds. It appeared to be under construction with new homes in different phases of construction.

Shortly after passing the old fairgrounds Rosalie and Christine noticed their backseat companion fade away as tears flowed down her cheeks. "Oh my," said Rosalie. "What happened to Violette?" "Alas," said Robert. "Time has passed and Violette has succumbed to her fate. There are all kinds of sicknesses throughout the world that doctors have not been able to cure. Many illnesses go undiagnosed or are improperly treated. In some circumstances there just isn't a cure or hospitals just lack the proper equipment. It is most common during these times."

Otto's sad voice explained. "Violette was only a child of 9 when she got a chest cold. At first she seemed ok but she deteriorated rapidly. She had difficulty breathing and was rushed to the hospital. We all prayed for her but I guess the Lord needed her with Him. The doctors said she had pneumococcal pneumoniae that lead to septicemia. To us it was just a lot of big words that took away this precious member of our family." It was hard for any of us to speak so for the rest of our trip we just folded our hands and bent our heads in prayer for Violette and others who had departed so early in their lives.

THE NEW ENGLAND FAIR

As we looked up our eyes gazed upon a wondrous site. We were passing the north side of Indian Lake and saw hundreds of people all dressed in their finest heading toward the banners and mayhem of the New England Fair. There were posters strategically placed all around the park. It appeared we were at the 1915 New England Fair. "With a slight smile, I turned to Rosalie and Christine. "Not only do we have to keep track of where we are, we really have to keep track of when we are." The buckboard stopped at a pavilion set up as a farmers' market. Off to one side was a booth with a large banner that read, "St. Ann's French Canadian Orphanage – Fruits, Vegetables and Flowers Grown with Hard Work and Lots of Love"

Otto leapt off the buckboard and quickly started to unload the vegetables in the back. We alighted the Buckboard and went over to visit the group of youngsters selling the fruits of their labor. What a glorious sight to behold. We tried to chat with them before we realized we were not a part of their lives. We were just a wisp of wind to them. So we had to be content on eavesdropping on their conversations.

"Loretta, would you please show Eva and Ester where to set up the vegetables that our friend Otto has brought to us from the farm." commanded Charles. "And Walter, would you help Harry build another platform. It seems we have plenty to sell this year."

"What a site to behold." whispered Christine. "Look at all these vegetables they have grown in their gardens." "What about all those beautiful looking flowers." said Rosalie. "Most of them have blue and red ribbons on them. It looks like they made a great showing at the flower show."

People meandered about the farm stand as they mulled over the quality of the produce. They picked the fresh fruits and vegetables and placed them into their baskets as quickly as the girls could set them onto the stands. An elderly lady remarked. "What lovely vegetables you children have here. You should all be proud of what you have accomplished." With that, she not only paid the asking price for the basket of food she had collected but gave them an extra payment for the orphanage. "Thank you so much." said Baby Ruth in her soft sweat voice.

Next to the farm stands were booths set up for locals to sell their home made foods. A group of girls were standing by a booth with Sister Nancy overlooking the operation. Joan yelled out. "Come and buy one of our delicious homemade pies. Come closer and take in all the amazing aromas. We have all kinds for you today. There are pumpkin pies, minced meat pies, fruit pies, custard pies and even a shepherd's pie. Don't miss your chance to taste one of our scrumptious pies. We make them with lots of hard work and so much love."

Ida began her spiel from the other end of the booth. "If you are not a lover of pies, I have for you a variety of canned and preserved goods. Come here and see our home made line of canned vegetables, tomato pasta sauce, and an assortment of canned fruits. Next to our canned goods we have jars of preserves and jellies. Stock up today for the long winter ahead."

"Good afternoon, one and all. Please don't forget our large assortment of cakes." Bellowed Olivia from another part of the large booth. "Chocolate cakes with whipped cream topping. White cakes with our special yellow colored frosting. There are many other cakes for you to choose. Don't forget to buy one of our Boston Cream Pies, which is really a cake."

"We make it the same way the original Parker House Chocolate Cream Pie has been made since 1856. Look at this French butter sponge cake filled with crème pâtissière that oozes out between the layers. A little brush of rum syrup and some sliced almonds brings out the unique flavor. Let's not forget the top coating of chocolate fondant. It makes my mouth water just talking about it. This beauty was entered in the competition and won the first place blue ribbon for best cake at this year's fair."

Robert waved to us to follow him as he headed for another part of the fairgrounds. As we were walking along the paths we saw amazing things, even for us. What we perceived as something old was just a new revelation during this era of invention. Up in the skies we witnessed the aerobatics of an antique looking plane. Christine made the first observation. "It reminds me of the time we went to the Smithsonian Museum in Washington, DC where we saw the Wright Brothers 1909 military plane."

More people glanced skyward as the plane flown by aviator William Luckey started what seemed to us like insane maneuvers for such a flimsy aircraft. "Look at that crazy man." Yelled an onlooker. "Isn't that the most incredible thing you've ever seen?" Others in the area gathered in his group and watched the show in awe.

"I heard that tomorrow they are having hot air balloon rides. I'm on my way to get a ticket before they run out." Another man added. "I was talking to a gentleman who said that some men were going to jump out of that hot air balloon with something they call a parachute." Someone else said. "Well, that parachute thing better be big and soft or there'll be quite a mess." They all chuckled and continued their observation of the acrobatic spins above them.

We walked into the animal holding enclosures of the Fair. It looked like they were done with the judging. There was a group of animals from St. Ann's Orphanage being corralled into their transports by a group of boys and a few men. Luther turned to his brothers Essex and James, "Make sure the chickens are properly set in their coops. It looks like our first prize Rhode Island Red will be strutting his stuff about the farm." Almost all the animals had colored ribbons draped upon them. "Our fine looking farm animals really did themselves proud."

We could still understand what the animals were saying. Their chatter was of jubilance as each holder of a ribbon proudly pranced about. Some bragged more than the others. But all-in-all each and every one of them had a great showing at the fair. Again, the St. Ann's family outdid themselves.

"Wooh-erk Wooh-erk. Look at me with my blue ribbon." crowed Rudy, the Rhode Island Red. "Hey, Flora, that red ribbon looks good on you. I see you did a great job showing your stuff too Renee. That's my girls."

Edna, the ewe, bleated out as loudly as she could. "Heyyyyy, look at my kids Nelson and Eddie. They have handsome yellow ribbons. There's my cute little lambs, Mary and Sandy. They won third place white ribbons that match their beautiful coats."

"Oink-Oink, we did pretty well too. Porky, Dorky and, oh yah, me, Morky are bringing home red, white and pink ribbons. We are surely making St. Ann's pig sty a drift to recon with."

"Hey guys, mooed Rita, did you hear? Charlie Junior took second place in last night's horse trotting race. I'm sure Sally the mare is very proud of him."

"Did you see me out there?" Purred Lola Bee. "If it wasn't for me Joker would have gone home without a ribbon. After he did all his macho fetches and tricks I figured he needed a little help in the Fancy Dancy Prancing Circle. Turns out I was right. The judges didn't notice Joker until I pounced on his back and we showed them what team work was all about. We both got an honorable mention for my ingenuity."

We kept moving through the fair ground as there was still so much to see. "Hey Rosie, Chris," I said. "Did you guys take a good look at the posters placed about the fair? This fair is unbelievable! Besides having war planes dropping bombs and doing their fancy flying there will be an auto show and an industrial exposition. During the day time they are having horse shows and flower shows."

"Oh," said Rosalie. "I heard one of the boys back there talking about St. Ann's getting a bunch of first prize ribbons at the flower show." Robert piped in, "I'm sure Pepere, I mean Ernest, has a great big smile on his face."

Christine spoke next. "I saw a poster that said during the evenings they were going to have horse trotting races, a car race and even athletes racing. They are also going to have fireworks just before closing. These fairs seemed to be a lot better than the ones we've been to." "Well, said Robert. "unfortunately for us the children can't stay after dark. We must get back for prayers and to prepare for our evening meal."

We entered a large open aired canopy that was headlined as 'The Biggest Ever Vaudeville and Mid-Air Show Assembled

Under the Blue Canopy of Heaven'. Inside we witnessed all sorts of vaudeville acts and stage shows. We even saw a performance group from St. Ann's Orphanage. The children were wonderful. Afterward they went about the crowd collecting donations. "Alright." commanded Loraine, one of the older girls who was put in charge of the troop. "Get together with your partner and head out to the buckboard. Mister Robert has no time to delay. It is getting late and we must move along quickly. Helen and Darlene, make sure the little ones are safely seated in the back of the buckboard." All the children instantly did as they were told.

IT'S HARD TO SAY GOODBYE

Once the children filled the back of the buckboard we headed back toward the orphanage. Otto turned and faced Christine and Rosalie. He looked much older than when we first met him. Obviously time was constantly changing. "Would you like to hear my story? It too is a story of sadness and woe." "Of course we would." said Rosalie. Otto continued. "My mom passed away with consumption when I was very young. St. Ann's Orphanage became my home until I was old enough to take care of myself.

I worked hard while living there. My chores, like most of the boys, was to learn all about farming and care of the gardens. I especially liked tending to the flower garden. It seemed like every day I was in the garden a presence was guiding me. I know now that it was old man Ernest who took me under his wing, so to speak."

"This fair would be my last one as I was of age to leave the orphanage. Soon after my departure I wed a lovely young lady. We both went to Holy Cross College. I was going to learn all there was about horticulture. Within three years Susie and I had two children, William and Blanche. I didn't complete my studies since a call to arms was issued by President Woodrow Wilson."

"It seemed that isolationism in the United States had come to an abrupt end. Many of our citizens were being killed by the Germans. War was declared on April 2, 1917. By the middle of June, I was one of 10,000 troops ordered overseas. We were now part of the 'War to End All Wars'."

I could feel him getting anxious so I put my arm around his shoulder. He paused to take a deep breath before continuing. "About a year later my combat infantry was outside a small village in the north of France. We were under heavy enemy fire when I was struck down by a German bullet." He pointed to a bloody hole appearing in the middle of his chest. Tears started flowing down my cheeks as I strengthened my hug. As he faded away we could barely hear his last words. "It is a bit ironic. You see, that small village was where my great grandparents grew up. My life has come full circle." With that Otto faded away, leaving me with empty arms. A deep sadness overcame us as our tears freely flowed. We again sat there in silent prayer.

As we made our way to the top of Vernon Street, we noticed some of our passengers in the back of the buckboard were fading away and new faces were taking their places. We realized we were still passing through time. This continued as we approached our destination on Granite Street.

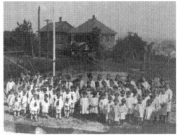

When we arrived at St. Ann's French Canadian Orphanage we saw smoke billowing from one of the structures south of the main building. Robert pulled the reins to stop the buckboard and turned toward us. "Please, my friends, run into the building and give the alarm. Our barn is on fire."

As soon as we jumped off the transport Robert slapped the reigns and sped toward the barn. Without hesitation we ran through the doorway to sound the alarm. Upon entering the building, we felt a sense of calm come over us. It appeared we had made the jump into another time period. "Did you guys feel that rush come over you too?" asked Christine. "Wow." Said Rosalie. "My equilibrium just turned upside down. I feel the alarm has passed, too." I said. "We may as well look for our next encounter." So off we went in search of what was to come next on our incredible journey.

Chapter 4

The Roaring Twenties

BRICK IS IN AT ST. ANN'S ORPHANAGE

As we turned down a narrow corridor a familiar figure showed herself to us. Saint Bernadette was again in our presence. "Bonjour, mes amis. Are you enjoying your journey, so far?" "Mais oui!" said Rosalie as if French was coming back to her. "I hope it has been an enlightening one." "Enlightening is one of many words we could use." I said. "Thank you so much for allowing us the opportunity to see all these wondrous things."

The passageway had large pipes and cast iron radiators mounted along the wooden walls. Old flower patterned curtains hung in the windows on both sides. "I remember this." said Rosalie. "This is the hallway that connected the old wooden building to the brick building." Saint Bernadette turned and smiled at her. "You see, my friends, your memories are stronger than you think."

Into the brick building we went. "Where are you taking us?" asked Rosalie. "Your memories were much stronger in this building." said Bernadette. "So here is where I will send you on your next phantasmic rendezvous." We were escorted into a large chamber that had a sea of small white iron beds. At almost the same instant Rosalie and I spurted out, "Yah, I remember this place!" Saint Bernadette had also vanished in that same instant.

I guess we were getting used to this happening and paid it no mind. We walked about the room going down the pathways between the beds. "The beds look so small." said Rosalie. "So many unpleasant memories happened in this big room." "I'm sure even the children of this time had bad memories here." said Christine. "Besides that, any child going to bed would have time to reflect on what happened to them and their families." "Yes," I said. "This would have to be the saddest place in the orphanage."

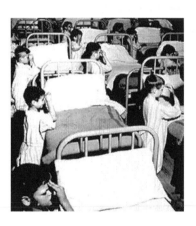

The beds were neatly made up and everything looked like new. About midway through our walk about the beds I thought I heard sobbing. Christine and I turned to see Rosalie sitting on one of the beds slowly rubbing her hands across the pillow. She said. "Sourier, you'll find that life is still worthwhile if you just smile." She got up and with a tear in her eye she smiled. We continued our walk through the sea of beds.

Since there was no specter to greet us we walked over to the far side of the room. We looked into a small bedroom in the far corner of the room. It was where a nun would spend the night while making sure the children did not get into any mischief. It was also her duty to take care of the sick children in the infirmary. Adjacent to the bedroom was a single bathroom which was obviously meant for her. Connected to it was another single bathroom. As we passed through it we realized it was for the infirmary which was the next room.

We walked out of the infirmary back into the dormitory and looked into the next room along that wall. It was set up as a sewing room. It seemed logical since most of the clothes had to be made or mended. We proceeded to the other side of the dormitory and entered what looked like a huge closet. Along each wall were cubby holes with clothing in them. Each one had a number.

I said, "With kids coming and going, I'm sure it was easier for the nuns to just call out a number than to remember your name. I'm glad I don't remember my number."

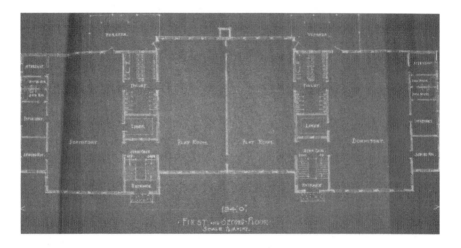

We moved along to the next doorway and went into a much larger room toward the back of the dormitory. "Oh, the toilets." I said as I turned to one side and pointed to two rows of five commodes facing each other from opposite walls. "Side by side with a little barrier between them and face to face. Absolutely no privacy. Even to this day I hate going into a men's room that has more than one toilet."

I turned to the other side of the room and said. "Look there, the sinks are also within view of the toilets. This place still gives me the creeps." There were two pathways for the sinks. In one pathway, there were six side by side sinks on each side. The other pathway had a row of six sinks and opposite them were two large tubs and a maintenance sink.

Opposite the dormitory entrance to the toilets was another entryway. Passing through it brought us into this great room that extended from the front to the back of the building just like the dormitory did. "It looks like this is one big play room." Said Christine. "It was that and more." I replied. "As you can see, the room is set up so some of the kids could sit around those tables to study their school assignments. Over there, you can see the play area where others would play games and carouse about."

Rosalie added. "You know this building was built so that the north side was a mirror image of the south side. And don't forget the second floor was a duplicate of the first. The younger children stayed here on the first floor and the older ones stayed on the second floor."

"Well," said Christine. "Let's not forget the basement floor." At least once a week, unless otherwise needed, the children would be gathered in a group of about 20 or so and marched down the hallway steps, with a face cloth and bar of soap in hand, to the shower room. It was just that, a large open room with 26 shower heads ready to deploy what was hoped to be warm water upon them."

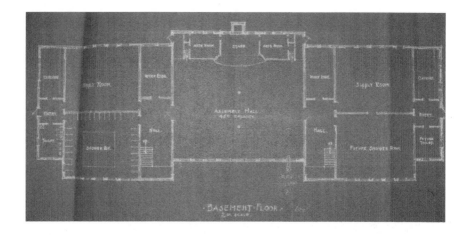

Christine continued talking as we made our way down the stairs to the lower level. "Decency was a must, so the girls would wear terry cloth robes into their shower room while the boys would wear what looked like baggy white cotton shorts into theirs. I'm sure almost all the kids who showered in those quarters remembered. I heard that one time the boys had to sing Amen, Amen, when they took showers because they had been fooling around so much."

"If I remember correctly, there was a large supply room in the back of the building. There it is. The nuns had a lot of stuff stored in here. The children had to walk through it to get to the side entry hallway. When they came in from the outside they had to hang their coats and stuff in the large closet room on one side of the entryway. There was also a toilet just inside the doorway so they didn't have to go all the way upstairs."

"Hey Rosie," I said, as we moved into a large room in the middle of the basement. It was the assembly hall that held about 450 people. "Now this is the place I remember very well. I'm sure we performed many times up on that stage. Many people and family members came here to watch us perform. Each Christmas Santa would come here and give the children presents."

It seemed no different than most auditoriums. The stage in the center and stairs leading up to the ante rooms on each side. In the far corners were short hallways leading to exit doors.

As we approached the stage two figures emerged from the ante rooms. "Ladies and gentleman." "Called out the male figure. "Welcome to the newest addition to St. Ann's French Canadian Orphanage. My name is Clarence. This young lass is my friend Peggy. We are your guides into the 'Roaring Twenties'. Please take your seats as we present 'The Roaring Twenties – St. Ann's Style'." It looks like we were in for a stage show, like no other we have seen.

ACT 1 – IN LIKE A LION

Clarence moved to a podium, stage left, while Peggy did the same, stage right. He began his narration. "The year is 1921. The new barn is already being built after the old barn was badly damaged in a recent fire." On his side of the stage we could see a mock barn being built. "The cost to rebuild was $16,500, quite a good some in those days." Children started moving about the stage in front of a large painted back drop depicting the farm hands. "The children of St. Ann's French Canadian Orphanage would continue working the farm while the sisters and novices went about Worcester soliciting funds to help defray the costs."

The voice of Peggy rang out from her podium. "Look, entering the orphanage is a woman with her three young children." We turned our heads to her side of the stage. "Let us listen in to a story that is been told so many times to the Grey Nuns." Our view of the stage seemed to be zooming in as we followed the young mother and her children. They entered a large sitting room where the sister superior and an assistant sister and novice greeted them.

One of the older girls, named Alice played the young mother. "Sister Superior, I come here with a heavy heart and in need of your help. My husband, Harley passed away during the influenza pandemic. I have tried so hard these past years to care for my children but find it too much to bear. We no longer have a home of our own and I cannot work and care for my children at the same time. I have no choice but to give them into your care." "We understand your situation." replied the Sister Superior, played by Doris. "We have many children living here who have encountered the same fate as your children."

"We must enter your family information into our log. We need your name and the names of your children." "I am Alice. The mother of Susan, Florence and Emile. When I am back on my feet can I return to take my children home?" Sister Suzanne, replied. "That all depends on whether or not we can find an adoptive home for any one of them. If a child is in our care long enough, or payment is not forthcoming, he or she may be placed for adoption. If that happens, you cannot get them back. Therefore, you must do your part to maintain support for your children during their stay. Once you do get work catch up on overdue payments and pay their boarding fees on time. We also ask that you visit them often." The lights on the stage slowly dimmed.

Peggy's narration continued. "The influenza pandemic of 1918 took the lives of nearly 45,000 people in Massachusetts. That's nearly four times the number of men that died in WWI from the entire six New England States. Other families were displaced by illnesses like diphtheria and tuberculosis. Orphanages were being filled quickly during the early 1920's. But, the 1920's also brought prosperity and good times to the fortunate ones of the world."

"That's right Peggy." said Clarence. "We can't forget how the Roaring Twenties also affected St. Ann's Orphanage." The stage behind him transformed into a scene from a speakeasy. Music from the era played in the background as girls and boys danced on stage. "My friends, let us listen in to the conversation the young couple, sitting at the back corner table, are about to have." With that introduction we turned our attention toward them.

"Victor, I have bad news to tell you." "Sal, how bad can it be? This is the best years of our lives. The economy is great, the stock markets are climbing higher every day making us lots of money, and we have found the best speakeasy in town. What could ever be bad news?" "Oh Victor, I am in a bad way. I am with child." Victor was taken aback and showed concern. "Oh Sal, what are we going to do? We aren't married and are catholic. We can't just 'get rid of the thing'." After a slight pause of thought he said. "Why don't we give it to the orphanage?" "What a great idea." beamed Sal. "They should be able to find a nice family who wants a baby. That way we can continue to have this great life we have without the burden of a child." Victor leaned over the table to give Sal a kiss and said. "That's why you're 'My Gal Sal'." The stage lights slowly went to dark.

Peggy provided a final comment. "Up to now orphans were from broken homes. Death of a mom or dad was the main reason children were placed in orphanages. The Roaring Twenties brought about a large influx of another type of orphan, the unwanted child."

ACT 2 – FINANCIAL HELP NEEDED, FAST

Clarence began the next narration. "Ladies and gentlemen, it has come to our attention that a serious predicament is about to unfold at St. Ann's Orphanage." The stage lights are turned up and we see some men talking with some nuns. The scene shows them walking between small beds in one of the dormitories. One of the men speaks. "Sister Superior, we have completed our inspection of your property and have bad news. The Board of Public Safety has declared the top floor of this 4-story wooden structure unsafe as a residence in which to house the children."

"Oh my Lord." answered Sister Superior. "What does this mean for the orphanage?" "It seems you have little choice. The Board will only allow the children to stay here for a short period of time to allow you to find some way to house these orphans. But you must act quickly or the orphanage will be shut down and the children relocated." The men walked off the stage.

The nuns gathered into a group as Sister Superior began giving orders. "Sisters, we knew this day was at hand. We must now act upon this situation quickly. Sister Janet, set up a meeting with our newest benefactor, The Orphans Friend Society. Sister Sandra, you must contact the Community Chest. It is time we became a member. We will need to start receiving funds through the annual Golden Rule Drive and Red Feather drive. If we do not get support from these and other benefactors, we will have to close our doors to all these children in need." The stage lights again dim.

Peggy completes the narration. "Here we are, inside this grand building. It wasn't easy, but somehow, $160,000 dollars was begged for and borrowed. This large four story brick dormitory was quickly constructed and now up to 250 children would have a place to sleep. It conformed to strict fire regulations and was built behind the older wooden building. A bridge corridor connected the two buildings. After major repairs, the older building continued to be used as a school, chapel, kitchen and dining room."

ACT 3 – DON'T FORGET THE CHILDREN

Clarence looked up to the audience. (That's us.) He talked in a solemn voice. "Now, let us not forget the children." The lights again were turned up to reveal a girls' dormitory with young girls laying in their white colored iron beds. "Jeanne," whispered Dotty. "Stop your crying. The sister will hear you. So take your hands out from under the covers or she will punish you for your mischievousness." "Oh, Dotty. I miss my mom so much. The nuns don't seem to care that I am so sad and separated from my family." "Shhhh, keep your voice down or we'll all get into trouble." Said Lilly.

Jeanne continued to whimper. "I know my brothers are here but the nuns won't let me see them. I feel so alone. Doesn't anyone love me anymore?" Hey kid," blurted Lilly. "You're stuck in this orphanage whether you like it or not. We all lost everything when we came here. The nuns only care that we be good little girls." "That's right." said Dotty. "All we can do is look out for each other. None of these grownups will. Now, please, go to sleep. Dream about when you get older and finally get out of this place. Then you won't have any one to push you around anymore. It may not be much, but it will make you feel a tiny bit better."

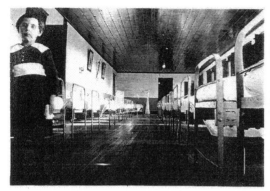

"Ok." said Vivian from two beds over. "Let's get some sleep. We have to get up early tomorrow. It's ironing day and you know those irons are going to be hot and heavy. The older girls and sisters won't be too happy if they don't have hot irons ready for them when the laundry is done."

With tears in our eyes of days gone by we turned to the podium where Clarence made his closing remark. "No one said 'Good-night' since they all knew there would never be a good night for them. For most, these feelings would last a life time." Darkness consumed the stage once more.

ACT 4 – OUT WITH A BANG!

Peggy was about to begin speaking when, suddenly, BANG!! We heard sometime crash upon the stage. We assumed one of the stage sets had fallen during preparation for the next act. The lights shone brightly upon the stage and we could now see what looked like a major city scape. Actors were jumping out of building windows pretending to commit suicide. People were running in and out of the banks. Complete mayhem was being depicted before us. A street sign became clear to us. It was Wall St.

"Look there." said Rosalie. "It's Wall St. This must be the Market Crash of 1929. They seem to be in a bit of a panic, don't they?" I added. "Many people killed themselves during those first few days. All those rich folks from the Roaring Twenties got a bit too cocky. They thought their money would just grow and grow. It's kind of like gamblers putting all their money down on one roll of the dice. Reality, I guess, will always bite you in the ... Sorry, I got carried away."

"It's just like these kids." said Christine. "Their 'Reality' is living day to day feeling abandoned and without love, not knowing when they will get out of those orphanages. How can anyone not feel sorry for them." Peggy called out from the stage. "It seems like the rich have been put in their place for the time being, but the future for the middle class is poverty. What about the poor? Is there such a place called below poverty? Of course there is. It's called dirt poor and homeless."

The stage background faded away as Clarence and Peggy met at center stage and held hands. Clarence provided the last words of the program. "As the lights dim for one last time we would like to thank you for coming to our show. The Roaring Twenties did come in like a lion and went out with a bang. We ask that our guests retire through the exits on either side of the stage."

They gave one last bow, turned and departed into the ante rooms from where we first saw them enter the stage.

As we solemnly walked toward the exit I said. "It looks like our next step into St. Ann's Past will be the 1930s. You guys better prepare yourself. I'm guessing this decade is going to show us a new wave of inhumanity. If you remember your history lessons you'll remember the 1930s was a decade of unemployment, poverty and humiliation for many of the working class people."

Rosalie said. "I bet there's going to be a bit more to it when you talk about orphanages and the 1930s in one sentence." "Well," said Christine. "Let's get to it. I think this will be the most eye opening decade of them all." So out the door we went as we wondered who would be our brave guide for our next enlightenment?

Chapter 5

Depressed & Angry

WHAT DID WE DO TO DESERVE THIS?

As we egressed from the stage doors we were welcomed by a teen aged girl and a boy that was about twelve years old. "Come quickly or you'll miss it." Rambled Margaret as she took hold of Rosalie. "Paul, take hold of Ms. Christine's arm. We don't want her falling. We must go to the main building." "Whoa, slow down." I said. "We don't want anyone getting injured." I'm sorry sir. It is important that we get you there on time."

OK, we were intrigued and moved as quickly as possible. Around the brick dormitory we went and up the slope to the older wooden building. We followed our guides into the Bowman Wood annex and into a large meeting room we had previously been in before. A father and mother were there with their two children. We knew what was about to happen. Another displaced family would leave their children not knowing the life time ramifications of such a decision. All we could do was stand to the side and watch it all unfold before us.

Sister Superior looked at the shattered and torn clothed family and sternly asked. "Why are you here? I see before me a man and his wife with no physical disabilities. Mr. Belanger, is this not your wife and two children standing beside you? I don't understand why you are bringing your children to us?" "Sister

Superior," Replied John Belanger. "You must understand our situation. We do not make this decision lightly. Anna and I dearly love Frederick and Henrietta so very much. But we need to ask that you take them in as borders only long enough for us to find work and get back on our feet."

"What makes you think we can support your children? Our beds are filling to capacity. Just because we are an orphanage doesn't mean we have money growing on trees. We have to go out just like you do and beg for it." She paused for a second or two, and took a deep breath. "Fortunately for you, we are sworn to take in all those in need. So we will take your children."

The children started to cry and begged their parents not to do this. "Stop your whining children. There'll be none of that here. Do you understand?" The children nodded. "Mr. & Mrs. Belanger, I suggest you have a good talk to your children before you go. It is important in this house that ALL the children do as they are told. There will be no exceptions. We don't have time to coddle every single child we have here."

"One more thing before you go. This is not a free ride we are giving you. You are both capable of working and must help provide for your children's care while they are here. Once you find a job you must immediately start paying for their room and board. The cost is a fair one. Also, the weekends are set aside for family visits." Sister Superior handed a paper to Mrs. Belanger. "Here are the weekly charges and the hours you may visit. Now let us get your information entered into our log book."

As the log book was being filled in Sister Vicieux turned to the children. With a stern voice she said, "You, Frederick, here is a label with the number B234 on it. This is your number. You will memorize this number and never forget it. It is an easy one, so I do not want to hear that you forgot it. Henrietta, your number is G52. The same goes for you."

"When you get to your dormitory you will be shown the cubby closet. You will look for the cubby that has your number on it. That will be your cubby. You will get your daily clothing from this cubby. Your clothes will be marked with your number. You will wear only your numbered clothing unless told otherwise."

Sister Superior intervened. "We have all the papers completed so it is time for Frederick and Henrietta to be on their way to the dormitories to get cleaned up. We believe that a clean child is a Godly child."

She turned to Sister Grace and waved her hand toward the doorway. Sister Grace knew exactly what to do. With a calming voice she said, "Come on, you two, off we go." The children jumped into their parents' arms and wept uncontrollably. "Go children." sobbed Anna. "Be good. The sisters will take good care of you. We will see you soon." They slowly walked out of the room with Sister Grace all the while hearing their parents profess their love.

Once the children disappeared from view John and Anna Belanger made their way toward the door. Anna turned one last time and begged. "You will take good care of them, won't you? Sister Superior responded. "We take good care of all the children."

Our guide, Margaret, waved for us to follow Sister Grace into the hallway. We paused long enough to hear the other sisters in the room make some comments. "It looks like our numbers will quickly exceed the 250 beds we are holding." Another replied. "It looks like this new group of kids are really going to give us problems. We must be extra firm with all of them. Spare the rod and spoil the child. We must take immediate command of them." Sister Vicieux stood up and made her way to the door. "I'll go and help Sister Grace. We should get started right away."

Our other guide, Paul, pulled on Christine's arm and said. "Come, Ms. Christine, we don't want to miss this." So we heeded his request and followed them through the hallways, over the enclosed walkway between the two buildings and into the brick dormitory. We caught up to Sister Grace handing over Frederick to Sister Vicieux.

"How old are you, boy?" demanded Sister Vicieux. "T-t-t-ten." Sputtered Frederick. "That's 'Ten, Sister Vicieux'. Do you understand?" "Y-y-y-es, Sister Vicieux." She gave him a smack across the back of the head and said. "Up and over we go then. You earn a bed with the big boys." Sister Grace turned away and walked Henrietta into the lower girls' dormitory since she was only 7 years old.

As they departed we turned to Margaret and Paul in search for some answers. Rosalie Asked. "What happened during the 1930s? It seems that by the end we see all kinds of bad things going on." Paul started first. "For many years St. Ann's had up to 250 kids living together. There have been stories that with this new group of kids the nuns couldn't handle the anger these kids had. They no longer feared the strap or stick. Some even thought if the boys remained as teenagers there would be fooling around, if you know what we mean."

"We do." said Christine. "I heard the boys were either sent back to their homes or sent off to a boys' reformatory school when they were 12 or 13 years old. So the sisters weren't going to take any chances. They could handle the young girls, but not the growing boys."

Margaret added. "No matter how much punishment the nuns dished out the boys became stronger and angrier. When puberty set in a lot of the boys flexed their muscles and rebelled. This is what convinced the nuns to send the boys off at such an early age." "That's true." Said Paul. "My friend Edward was just sent away and I'm supposed to go back home to my mother next week. We are both twelve years old."

"Listen." I said. "I think I hear an alarm. Do you guys hear that?" Christine replied. "I do. It's coming from the old building." "We must hurry." said Paul. "Let's get to the front of the building along Granite Street." We all hurried making sure we were not separated. We crossed Granite Street and stood in front of the Grotto. We could see the South side of the white wooden building bellowing smoke out the roof top. Fire engines seemed to appear from both ends of Granite Street. I said. "This must be the Christmas fire from Dec. 27, 1939. Am I correct?"

Margaret pointed while speaking. "Yes Mr. Joe. It was reported to have started in a lower floor rubbish shoot and quickly moved up the shoot to the roof. Some rooms connected to the rubbish shoot were damaged. Fortunately, this was the Christmas holiday week and most of the children were away visiting families or taken in by friendly people living in and around Worcester. The 60 or so children still here were in the brick dormitory building safe from the fire. It has yet to be confirmed or denied that old records and entry logs from the orphanage were also lost or destroyed during this fire."

SCENE OF FIRE IN ORPHANAGE

"Many think this was the worst thing to ever happen to St. Ann's Orphanage. That is not so. By the end of the 1930s this establishment had become an unhappy and militaristic place. Children were no longer defined as 'the children that came here because they lost their mom and dad in a car crash', or as 'the children that were abandoned', or even as 'the children that were left here because of necessity'. They were only defined as 'the children that needed constant reinforcement of the rules'. Their first day consisted of a welcoming punishment to insure the child knew his or her place. Humiliation would be used as a tool to force children not to do things the nuns did not approve. I could go on, but you will hear more of this from future specters you will encounter."

Paul concluded. "In the orphanage, the 1930s was not about eating the new goodies sold at the market. You wouldn't find a Hostess Twinkie, a Snickers Bar or Wonder Sliced Bread here. FDR once said. "You have nothing to fear but fear itself." Tell that to a child who only sees a depression far worse than what is outside the walls of this institution. Come we must bring you back to the play room. The show is about to start." We tried to ask what he meant but there was no answer. All we could do at this point was quickly follow Paul and Margaret.

Chapter 6

Radio Flyer

THE NEWS – HOME AND AWAY

Across the covered hallway into the new brick dormitory building we went. Up a flight of stairs and left into a large play room. We walked over to where a group of girls were gathered in front of an old radio. Or at least to us it was an old radio. It was a large upright piece of furniture placed along the center wall. It surely reminded us of the old 78rpm juke box our stepfather once had in our home. Behind the girls were three chairs. A young girl waved us over. "Bonjour, my name is Thomasina. I will be your hostess while you are entertained. Would you like a cup of tea?" We all replied, "Thank you, please." We sat down just in time to hear the opening of a local radio news show.

'Dateline: June 21, 1941 Worcester's own Local Weekend News: A look back on this past week: St. Ann's French Canadian Orphanage celebrated its 50th anniversary observance of its founding. Last Sunday started with a pontifical mass at St. Joseph's Church. Besides the hundreds of former residents of St. Ann's were numerous benefactors and special dignitaries from the Catholic Diocese of Springfield. The first sister superior, Sister Anna Piche, celebrating her eightieth birthday. also came to the celebration. The afternoon dinner brought nearly 1,000 celebrants to the orphanage. Other events included a picnic on the orphanage grounds, a stage play of the orphanage's history enacted by the children and an open house where hundreds of alumni made the pilgrimage back to the place they once called home.'

Thomasina arrived with the tea tray. "Here is your tea. I have provided milk and sugar on the side so you can make it to your satisfaction. I have included tea biscuits and short bread if you so desire." We all thanked Thomasina for her hospitality. "If you have any questions, please feel free to ask me. I am honored to stay with you." With that the radio volume increased and we could hear the introductory theme song of a radio show.

THE ORPHAN FANNIE RADIO SHOW

Theme song ending:
'Who's that little nosy girl?
The one with the twisty curl.
Whom do you see?
It's Little Orphan Fannie.'

Announcer: 'Here it is, 5:45 now and time to hear the new adventures of Little Orphan Fannie.'

'But first, if there is any of you boys and girls who don't like to drink milk and your mother scolds you because you don't drink enough, don't forget what a wonderful help Groovy Bean chocolate drink can be for you. Our friends Simon and Garfield say it best. Right Guys?' 'Right Mr. Announcer. (Singing the jingle) Groovy Bean outdoes the rest. That is why it's America's best!' – then the sound of Garfield slurping the empty drink with his straw.

Announcer: 'Thanks Guys. Now let's take a look at today's Little Orphan Fannie episode called 'Della's Story'. The day starts with a new boarder entering the dormitory. Like always, Little Orphan Fannie is the first one to greet the young girl.'

"Hey kid, what's your name?"

"Della."

"What brings you to our grand establishment?"

"My mom got sick with TB and my dad couldn't work and take care of us. So he went to the church we go to every Sunday but they told us they couldn't help us. They told him to send us to St. Ann's Orphanage."

"Sounds like you're not quite the orphan I am. You're what the nuns call 'Borders'. All you are good for is rent money your dad has to pay for you being here."

"But the Lord is supposed to help us find our way, not abandon us."

"Well kid, you will learn to pray here and follow the 'Golden Rule'. But, getting your prayers answered? Don't count on it. You're here to pray for forgiveness. Your soul has been tainted. You have become a burden to others and must do penance until you leave this place."

"Is that why I have to wear these clothes? Look at these things. I was given this black dress with a white stiff collar and cuffs, coarse feeling underwear and a long shirt. What's with these long black stockings and high buttoned shoes? Are we supposed to wear these all the time?"

"No, silly goose. Only when you go to church and when the nuns need you to impress their friends and benefactors." Suddenly Fannie's expression changed and she quickly turned and walked away.

"Do you know that nun who brought me up here? She slapped me for no good reason. All I was doing way crying because they separated me from my other sister and sent me in here."

Announcer: 'Suddenly the nun in charge of the dormitory grabbed Della by the back of the neck and told her to go and tell the Mother Superior that she was talking bad about one of the sisters. Punishment ensued leaving poor Della bruised, crying and confused. Nothing like that had ever happened to her before. She left the room with tears flowing and marks on her body hidden by her clothing. She didn't know what she was feeling. It was a mix of being scared, angry, embarrassed and all alone. Little Orphan Fannie greeted her as she returned to her bedside.'

"Hey kid, you alright?"

"No. Not only did she punish me more than the first nun did, but she gave me a chore to do every day. I have to sweep those wooden stairs in the other building with a small brush to loosen the dirt left behind by hundreds of shoes walking up and down on them. God has truly abandoned me. You were right when you said we do penance here."

"Della, at least there's a spark of hope. You may not see it now, but God does love you. Remember, he suffered for us. So I guess you can say, we must suffer for him. Someday your mom will get well and she and your dad will come for you. That is one hope a border has over an orphan like me. We, orphans can only hope that someday, someone will come and adopt us. In the mean time we just have to make the best of it."

Announcer: 'As we wait for time to pass by why don't you get up and run to your kitchen for a nice tall glass of Groovy Bean chocolate drink. Don't forget, Groovy Bean outdoes the rest. That is why it's America's best!' – 'Now let's look in on Little Orphan Fannie and her new best friend Della as they talk about the goings on at St. Ann's Orphanage.'

"Hey Della, why are you looking so sad? You've been here for a while now. You must have gotten used to this place by now."

"I'm sorry Fannie. There's not much to be happy about around here. I can't do anything right. I tried out for all kinds of parts for the Golden Anniversary play. But I'm just no good. While all the kids are practicing their dancing and singing, or rehearsing their lines in the historical play about St. Ann's I am stuck doing the extra chores they don't have to do."

"Yea, I know what you mean kid. There's a lot of stuff I'm doing for that thing."

"Well that's only the tip of my problems. I really can't get used to this place. I have no privacy. We share sleeping quarters in a room where 50 other girls sleep in small white iron beds that are crammed close together in lines and rows. Every day we get up out of bed at 5 am by the clanging of the nun's bell. I never had to do that before coming here. We have ten minutes, no longer, to get ready for the day. My shoes have so many buttons. They are so hard for me to put on and tie up. Many days my ears are red and sore after an impatient nun pulled them because I was too slow."

"Ha, tell me about it. I heard some of the girls got up early and tried to get dressed under the covers only to get caught."

"Well, guess what? I was one of them."

"Ouch!"

"As I said, the nuns didn't like me much so I was whacked all over my body, back, fingers, even my face. They would sometimes use a wooden spoon if they felt their bare hands weren't doing the job."

"Wow, I guess there were just some kids, like you, that the nuns just felt like torturing. Other than that, you must be getting used to your new life. The day to day goings on is run on a strict schedule here at St. Ann's. As you know the schedule is marked by the ringing of the bells and the sound of a nun's metal clacker. One clack to start two to stop and so on to let us know what is expected of us."

"Click clack, click clack. Fannie, those things are driving me insane! And what's with the numbers? The nuns here know me by my name, not my number. But a lot of the girls are just called by numbers marked in their clothes. Those cubby holes where we get our change of clothes is right next to that bathroom. You can actually see the girls going to the toilet while you're brushing your teeth. Eew, Disgusting! And we have to go all the way down to the basement to take a shower."

"Hey Della, what about them dreaded showers? Nothing like it that I know of. Who could ever imagine that a whole bunch of girls would be showering together? What an unpleasant experience. I guess for modesty sake they make us wear those silly looking garments when we shower. At least no one can see your scrubbed dry skin burning from the harsh brown soap we use. I also heard the boys have to sing that dreaded song, Amen, Amen, Amen."

"That's what I like about you Fannie. You tell it like it is. So what do you think about those Saturday rituals?"

"I guess that falls right into your hum-drums and woes, kid. As you know, after our group shower, we get dressed and graciously dawn our fancy clothes before assembling in the main room. In all the years I've been here nothing has changed except for the priest. There was Father Yvon Le Floc'h. Try to say that 5 times real fast! He left in 1939."

"We now have Father Alfred. Once his young flock has gathered he starts swinging that thurible of incense and chants in Latin, you know, the official language of the church. We may know French and English but Latin sounds pretty strange to me. Anyway, we proceed in a double line with the smallest child leading the rest of us thru the buildings to the chapel. On a good day the procession may even go outside before we enter the chapel."

"Fannie, there is no joy in this journey. It is solemn and sad. It emphasizes our uselessness and why we should never have God's love. The sermons are of hopelessness, and preach that we will never achieve goodness. No longer do I truly feel loved by God."

"It seems to me Della that you will certainly get into God's good graces. But you must give it time. Bear the brutality and you will be saved."

"It is so hard to bear. Nothing like this has ever happened to me. My mom & dad never treated me like this. So why do the sisters?"

"It's all about fear and control, Della. The sisters' cruelty and intimidation tactics are used to dominate us. We are being made to fear them. They control us totally, both physically and mentally. We must accept what they say. We have no other choice!"

"Well it's working. I can understand why some of the nuns do it. But some of the others seem to like being cruel and heavy handed. I think I'm picked on more because I can't do many of the things the other kids can do."

"Della, Della, Della. You are my best friend. I heartily believe, you will go home and be with your family once again. In the meantime, there are good things here. You'll see. I believe things will get better once this Golden Anniversary thing is done with. In the orphanage, none of us have very much. Unlike most kids on the outside we are rarely given candy. Once a month we may get to see a movie. Every so often we do go out on an excursion, like this Golden Jubilee. Just remember kid, the sun will shine tomorrow."

Announcer: 'Well kids, that does it for tonight's episode of Little Orphan Fannie. Don't forget to have your mom pick you up some of that delicious Groovy Bean chocolate drink. And don't forget, Groovy Bean outdoes the rest. That is why it's America's best!'

All the kids sitting around the radio began to clap and chatter amongst themselves. Rosalie, Christine and I had long finished our cups of tea and turned toward Thomasina who was still standing beside us. "That was quite a story Thomasina." "Yes, Mr. Joe. It sounded so much like our home here. The Golden Jubilee they mentioned was a big success. Nearly 1,000 people came to celebrate. It lasted an entire week." "Oh, please tell us about it." begged Rosalie.

"Lots of planning went into its preparation. I guess it really put a lot of pressure on all the sisters. Unfortunately for us kids that meant the pressure fell twice as hard on us." Christine interjected. "We are so sorry you kids had to endure that frustration." "Thank you mum. Most of the kids were getting used to it by the time the celebration started. Sunday, June 15, 1941 was the big day. Most of the nuns and a select group of us went to St. Joseph's Church for a pontifical mass. You wouldn't believe all the high level dignitaries that were there. That afternoon there was a grand luncheon hosted here, at St. Ann's Orphanage. Besides the priests and nuns, and all the benefactors, hundreds of former orphans and borders came."

"The rest of the week was also grand and the weather was nice and warm. Monday was all about the benefactors and people who helped out St. Ann's Orphanage. Tuesday was marked as 'Children's Day' with a picnic on the orphanage grounds. There was lots of food, games and fun to be had. This was one of those days, even for the shortest amount of time, you forgot about your woes and actually had a good time."

"Wednesday evening was 'History Recreated Night'. The big show of shows was put on by the children. Wow! You should have been there. What a gala event! All the children worked so hard and had the performances of their lives. Too bad they couldn't get a movie reel made of it. Anyway, Thursday was kind of a wind down day for the kids. Reverend Yvon Le Floc'h gave a memorial mass in our chapel in honor of deceased benefactors, nuns and alumni. Friday was the final day with an open house for everyone to come and visit. There were a lot of wet eyes as many former borders walked through the building remembering their days here."

"I am so sorry. I have rambled on too much. It is time for you to visit the boys' hall. Come with me."

"Thank you so much for the tea and the narrative about the Jubilee." said Rosalie as she gave Thomasina a big hug. "You are wonderful." Thomasina whisked us to the doorway adjoining the two large halls where we were to be introduced to our next guide, Donald.

THE 'IT PAYS TO BE CLUELESS' SHOW

As we passed thru the doorway into the boys' play room Thomasina vanished. The large hall was void of children. As with the girls' play room we could see three comfortable looking chairs waiting for us. In front of them was a desk with a vintage radio upon it. The radio was about 18" tall and 12" wide with a wooden casing. The front looked pretty fancy with the wooden grate over the speaker section. On the lower half of the radio were those old fashion knobs and dial. I guess this was considered a miniature radio in those days.

We sat down in our chairs and noticed the side table was already supplied with a pot full of tea and snacks. I made the comment. "It looks like our guide Donald has stood us up." "Yah, he probably had more important angel things to do than hang around with us." Said Rosalie. As we got cozy in our seats the radio turned itself on and voices were emanating from the speakers.

'We Break-in for a special news broadcast. FLASH... Washington... The White House has announced the Japanese have attacked the U.S Naval Base in Pearl Harbor, Hawaii. We now send you to Washington where President Franklin Delano Roosevelt is addressing the Senate and House of Representatives.

"Yesterday, December 7, 1941. A date which will live in infamy. The United States of America was suddenly and deliberately attacked by naval and air forces of the Empire of Japan..."

"Wow!" said Christine. "It really sends shivers up your spine when you actually hear him speaking live over the radio." "Bernadette did say we would really remember this experience." said Rosalie. The announcer returned to say. 'We now return you to your regularly scheduled program.'

Announcer: 'Good evening friends. Tonight's program 'It Pays to be Clueless' is going make you laugh and cry all at the same time. Guess what? Tonight we bring you the guy who claims to have seen it all at St. Ann's Orphanage. He was a border at that very orphanage here in our good city of Worcester, Massachusetts. But, before we introduce our good friend, Marcel Marsole, let's take a quick commercial break.'

Announcer: 'Hey there moms. Serve a breakfast you know your kids will love. Go to your pantry, take out that box of nutritious Quicker Oats. You know your kids can't wait to eat breakfast and you can have Quicker Oats in front of them in no time at all. Just use the supplied scoop from your Quicker Oats box, add two heaping scoops to a bowl, stir in a cup of hot water, then mix in milk and sugar to taste. Quick, delicious and good for you. What more could a mother ask for?' Now, without further ado, Marcel Marsole and 'It Pays to be Clueless'.'

As the canned applause filled the room Rosalie turned to Christine and said, "I've never heard of that radio show before." "I guess it wasn't one of the most memorable radio shows." said Christine. 'Good evening Ladies and Gentleman. What a great audience we have tonight. I was hoping for a bit more than three audience members, but tonight we are touching on a controversial subject that many folks don't like to discuss. That would be their time served at St. Ann's Orphanage.' I turned and whispered to Christine. "How does he know there's only three of us?"

'Why Mr. Joe, Marcel Marsole sees and hears all. This broadcast is specially formatted to be an informative broadcast suited for your listening and conversational pleasure.' "Does this mean we can talk and post questions to you and your guest?" 'Absolutely, Mr. Joe. But first let me bring on my guest of honor, Ivan A. Bandon. Like you folks and myself, Ivan has roots at St. Ann's Orphanage. We spent most of our time together. Let's give him a warm applause.' We actually clapped along with the canned applause emanating from the speakers.

'Hey Marcel. What's with the small audience? I wanted to tell the whole world how terrible that place was.' 'Well, Chip, you'll get your chance. This panel of listeners are going to be your conduit to the world. So this is your chance. Oh, sorry folks. You did hear me call Ivan 'Chip'. You see, I am the Ying and Chip is the Yang to these stories. I enjoyed my stay at St. Ann's where Chip despised his stay feeling quite 'abandoned'. Ivan A. Bandon really did have a 'Chip' on his shoulder.'

'For those folks who have listened to our show before, you know we always start our program off with a mini quiz. So, here is our first question: What do you call a kid in an orphanage? A. A Boarder – B. An inmate – C. A Resident – or D. All of the Above?' Chip quickly responds first. 'D. of course. It's always 'All of the Above'.' 'That was pretty fast Chip. Next time let's give the audience a chance to answer. OK?' 'Sorry.' 'I tell you what. Why don't we skip the quiz and get right to the stories? I'll start first. Then Chip, you can put in your two cents worth. Finally, our distinguished panel can ask a question or make a comment whenever they wish.' We all nodded in agreement.

'There are many reasons kids get sent to an orphanage. Mine is no different than a lot of kids. I was living not too far from St. Ann's Orphanage. I remember one time driving past it with my mom and dad. I was being a bit fussy sitting alone in the back seat complaining about not having a brother or sister to play with. My dad turned to me and said. 'Keep it up Marcel and we'll put you in that orphanage over there. There's plenty of kids you can play with. I hear they even give the kids a fresh orange if they are really good. Funny enough, I thought it would be neat. Little did we know that just a few months later my mom would get real sick and I would find myself living at St. Ann's. My dad had to pay $7 a week for the four months I stayed there.'

'Well, lucky you.' whimpered Chip. 'My mom wasn't a happy lady. My good for nothing dad was a no good drunk who drove my mom to an early grave. No sooner was she put to rest did he dump me off at this orphanage. We didn't have two nickels to rub together. He took off to places unknown and I never saw him again. So I became a non-paying inmate of this asylum. You bet I had to work twice as hard to pay for my keep.'

"Excuse me." interrupted Christine. I have read stories about boarders having to work in order to stay at St, Ann's. So, I guess this is not an unusual case. Right?" Marcel responded. 'That's correct Ms. Christine. Unless you were a true orphan, that is, unless you had no mom and no dad, you didn't have to pay for your room and board. Otherwise, as a boarder at St. Ann's Orphanage someone had to pay or work for their room and board.'

'That means, if you had a mom or dad one of them, or you, had to somehow work and pay for staying there. Over the years, women boarders would pay their room and board as cooks, dressmakers, teachers, or household servants. Men would pay their room and board as hired farmers, stable boys, and servants. Some older ladies paid a weekly fee or even willed their estates to St. Ann's so they could live there.'

"I guess that answers the question." said Rosalie. "Who am I? An orphan, a boarder, a resident, an inmate or 'All of the Above'." 'OK Folks.' said Marcel. 'I think it's time for a word from our sponsor.'

Announcer: 'Thanks Marcel. Men beware. Use one dab of Brylcream. Just a little dab makes your hair look excitedly clean, and disturbingly healthy.' Brylcream theme follows:

Brylcream, a little dab will do ya.
Brylcream, you'll look so debonair.
Brylcream, the gals will all pursue ya.
They'll love to get their fingers in your hair.'

Announcer: 'I got to say you look MARVELOUS!' With a big smile Marcel responded. 'Thanks Mr. Announcer. Let's get back to our panel discussion. Once I was dropped off at St. Ann's Orphanage things were quite different than what many people perceived them to be.'

'My first day there wasn't too bad. I remember seeing these stern looking nuns dressed in dark gray outfits. There was this big crucifix dangling from their necks. I thought for sure they would fall over from the sheer weight of them. All I could see was their faces. I was super polite when I met the nuns. I think they liked me. I was told that under no circumstances would I not follow

80

ALL the rules. If I did have an infraction I would be punished accordingly.'

'I thought to myself, "Big deal. They sound just like my dad. I'm sure I can take whatever they can dish out." So with a big smile on my face and my baby blues blinking away, one of the nuns quietly escorted me to the boys' dormitory. I just kept smiling, smiling, smiling.'

Chip butted in. 'You got to be kidding me! My dad dumped me off at the front door and told the nuns I was all theirs. Then my butt was dragged into some room where a group of them were gawking at me. I was scared to death. They knew it and they made sure I would stay that way. I've been scared ever since. Hah, nowadays even penguins scare the hell out of me.'

'All right Chip. Calm down. Let it go. There's plenty more stories to tell our guests.'

"You know Marcel. Chip does make a good point." I said. "We have read and heard all sorts of misgivings when a child is left in the hands of an orphanage."

'I dare to say that most, if not all, the stories you heard are true in nature. It's really about how the experience affected each individual child and family member. Not all parents were like Chip's dad. Most parents were desperate and placing their child here was only their last resort. In most cases the parent dearly loved their child. The horrible thing about this situation is the parents really didn't understand what kind of hell the child was going through.'

Rosalie intervened. "Oh my God, I know exactly what you're talking about. No one ever looked at it from our perspective. We were left alone, abandoned, frightened and scared to death. We had no idea what was going on. They expected us to immediately adjust to our new situation. For God's sake, we were just little kids! Our mom or dad could have just died, or even worse both of them. Our mom or dad could have gotten sick so they couldn't take care of us kids. The list goes on and on. Hundreds of different scenarios that could end up with a hapless child in the orphanage."

"Take Joe and I. We understand how Chip feels. Our dad liked the booze too. Our mom did the right thing after one too many whacks on the side of my head made me partially deaf. Divorce followed and our dad headed west. That meant our mom had to support herself. Therefore, into the orphanage we went."

"So you think you had it hard Chip? We were condemned children. My mom was excommunicated from the church since the church didn't believe in divorce. The nuns would remind us of this too. We would have to repent for our parents' sins. We would never be good enough for the Lord."

"OK Rosie, I said. "Remember, we need to 'Let it Go'. We know that we did nothing wrong. This was His way of pointing us in the right direction. One thing we can say is that a lot of kids went into St. Ann's broken. But a lot of us came out of St. Ann's stronger for our experiences there. We all have a different view on life than the ordinary child. I feel I have turned out a good person despite all the turmoil I went through. I'm sure many others would say the same thing. I think Marcel needs to continue with his other stories."

'Thank you Mr. Joe. Let me tell you the story of the...

Announcer: We Break-in for a special news broadcast. Dateline: June 6, 1944 Will forever be known as D-Day. More than 160,000 U.S. and allied troops landed on the beaches of Normandy, France. Gen. Dwight D. Eisenhower called the operation a crusade in which, "we will except nothing less than full victory." More than 5,000 ships and 13,000 aircraft supported the invasion. More than 9,000 allied troops were killed or wounded during the battle, but their sacrifice helped put Hitler and his Nazi regime back on their heels. God bless them, every one. We now return you to your local studio.'

'Wow, thank you Mr. Announcer for that great news. I guess time really does fly by quickly when you're having a great conversation. Alright, where was I? Ah, yes. Hey Chip, how's about we tell them the story of the pig in the poke?'

'You mean the Pokey Pig story? Why not? I'm sure they'll get a good laugh on my expense.'

'It's always about you, Chip. Isn't it? You don't have to answer. It's not all doom and gloom at the orphanage. Our good friends here look like they're ready for a fun story.'

'I guess we always thought of the nuns as delicate, but mean spirited. Well, the story goes, Bobby and his sister Mary snuck out early one morning and unlatched the gate to the pig pen. Holy-Moly! What a sight became of it all. Picture this; These weren't just three little pigs. We're talking huge hogs that looked the size of hippos! I don't know why they were raising them, but these nuns had the biggest hogs I've ever seen. Before long there were hogs running amuck through the fields, into the gardens and into the woods.'

'The alarm was struck and a large group of us kids were handed big sticks. Away we went running about the fields and into the woods. I think we spent more time laughing than herding. That ungodly sound. OINK-OINK. We would go one way and the hogs would go another. The nuns just stood back and screamed with laughter. I believe it was the first time I ever saw those nuns with such big grins on their faces.'

'All of a sudden, right in front of me was the biggest HOG I had ever seen. He came crashing through the corn field right toward me. I was scared out my mind as l looked into those mean eyes. He was going to trample me into human fodder. All of a sudden a sense of calm came over me as I swear I heard a voice command me to step aside. Without hesitation I obeyed, raised my stick and wacked that pig in the derriere as he rumbled on by. Even today I believe it was my Guardian Angel talking to me. Anyway, we eventually corralled them little rascals and sent them back to their pen.'

Chip chipped in. 'Like always, Marcel had a happy experience. You know it didn't end up well for me. I was ordered to man the pig sty gate and make sure the hogs didn't get out once they were put back in. Easier said than done. What is ever easy with me? As soon as one of those creatures got put inside it took one good look at me and stuck its muzzle where the sun doesn't shine and up and over I went. I swear the thing tossed me half way across the pen. SPLAT! Headlong into that pile of muck. Of course the hogs thought of me as one of theirs and helped insure every part of my body was covered. How that sludge got into places on my body I don't know. Grrrrr, I feel like I need a bath.'

Artwork by Soher Jesus Silva-Alvarado

'Well thank you Chip for your enlightening look into Hog Day at St. Ann's. I see our audience members have big smiles on their faces. That's why we do this. OK, let's listen to another story we all became part of. The beginning of a daily routine can really be trying for some kids. Let's talk about a story we have all been a part of, one way or the other. No real names here. Hypothetically, we'll use a boy named Larry.'

'It's early in the morning and the morning alarm sounds. That's the sister on duty. One of the boys loudly complains. "Damn! Who died and went to heaven?" Another boy retorts. "Whoever smelt it dealt it." Then the bantering began. "Whoever said the rhyme did the crime." "Whoever complained last set off the blast." said another.'

'The sister finally intervened. "All right you boys. Get out of bed, stand up next to them, remove your drawers and hold them out in front of you." That's right, we had to stand there naked with our... well, you get the picture. She proceeded up and down each row of beds until she stopped in front of Larry.'

'The poor kid was singled out in front of the entire dormitory. She pointed toward the boys' toilets and followed him in, bare butt and all. He was immediately placed in one of those big bath tubs where he soaked while all the boys came in to do their business, wash up and brush their teeth. Only when they were done was he able to get out of the tub and prepare for the rest of his humiliating day.'

'Poor hypothetical Larry.' said Chip. 'I feel for him. You see I, like a lot of boys and girls had a bladder problem when I was little. Some kids who woke up in the middle of the night were brave enough to sneak under the beds and worm their way into the toilets. But some of us didn't know what happened until we woke up to a warm, wet bed. You know we were humiliated beyond belief. It didn't matter that we had no control over what had happened. Off to the laundry we were paraded, holding our soiled clothes and bedding in our arms for all to see and smell. Over time, I think our anger over shadowed our humiliation.'

'What can I say Chip? There are so many things the kids had to endure. Anyway, let me continue our story of a typical day at St. Ann's. We got up out of bed, lined up, marched into the toilets and did your business. On to the sinks to wash up, brush our teeth and comb our hair. Click clack, click clack. Off we marched to the clothes closet to put on our outfit of the day. You find the cubby hole with your number on it and quickly change. There was no dilly-dallying here.'

'Then click clack, click clack, click clack. Off we went keeping in proper file. Marching through the building and over the connecting corridor into the main building and into the dining room where our morning feast awaited us. I tell you, this place surely prepared me for the 20 years I spent in the military.'

"Who could ever forget about the 'Bridge'." whispered Rosalie. "It was certainly part of everyone's daily routine."

'Now you have to remember this was war time. Half the canned goods in the U.S. were shipped overseas to our fighting men. We weren't desperate for food, but more than 200 kids are a lot of mouths to feed at any time. There was rationing going on. That meant imported things like sugar were rationed. It was mixed into our milk so that every one of us had sugar in our cereal. That meant sweet, soggy corn flakes, DELICIOUS! You can't think 'orphanage' without seeing kids chowing down on a thick, sweet bowl of porridge. YUCK! We sat down at our table and the nuns would walk behind us, lean over and slop up the meal of the day.'

"GIVE US THIS DAY..."

'Click clack, click clack. With breakfast done, off we marched to our morning assignment. "Hup two three four, over the bridge and through the door. Five six seven eight, stay in line and don't be late." Into the huge boys' play room we went where a sister in waiting handed out cloth pads to each of us. "Down you get boys. Today we make the floor shine as bright as the star over Bethlehem." The other boys fell down to their knees and started rubbing the floor. First the left hand, then the right hand. Back and forth they went. Not me! I slapped those soft pads under my shoes and started skating about the floor. "Swish, swash, swish, swash." Now that was fun.'

'The other boys saw how much fun I was having and before you knew it we were all going about making those swish, swash sounds. At first the sisters were appalled at the lack of discipline, but upon seeing the brilliant results they just stood back and watched in amazement. That was just another fun day at St. Ann's Orphanage.'

'From that day on all the wood floors were shined this way. All of us kids, boys and girls, actually looked forward to floor shining day. You know, someday I'm going to patent this. I'm going to put these pads on a stick and make the pads interchangeable for when you want to clean, dust or shine your floors. Hmmmm, I think I'll call it the SWISHER. What do you think Mr. Joe?'

I kind of chuckled and said. "Marcel that would certainly be something people in the future would want to have in their homes. If you can make something easy to use, you could have a great product. A great product would put you in the lap of luxury."

'Thanks, Mr. Joe. Is this luxury cute? Hah, only kidding Mr. Joe. I have plenty of ideas just like that. You know, my dad was right. He said if I did something good I might get an orange. The nuns liked my idea and that afternoon I was treated to an orange. It was so shiny and bright. I can still see it. Boy, it was so sweet and juicy. I tell you what. While I reminisce let's take this moment to hear from our news room and sponsors.'

Newsroom Reporter: 'War Update: Direct from our news headquarters. On May 8, 1945 England and its allies have declared

VE Day. Celebrations abound across the globe. Victory over Europe will be officially signed on May 16th. With Germany out of the picture we can now focus on taking down the Japanese Imperial Army. It seems the war will soon come to an end. We now return you to your local studio.'

The Announcer: 'Now a word from our sponsor.'

PEPSI COLA Jingle:
– Pepsi Cola hits the spot
– Twelve full ounces that's a lot.
– Twice as much for a nickel, too
– POP!
– Pepsi Cola is the drink for you.

The announcer returns: 'Now back to Marcel Marsole.'

'Thanks Mr. Announcer. Let's start by saying a silent prayer for all the men and women who have given their lives and those still fighting for all of us. While these brave souls were off fighting for us the women here didn't stand idly about. No sir. There were millions of them who worked in the ship yards and factories building the fighting machines and military equipment needed to win this war. Many more worked for our government and still more worked from their homes. All of them helping to get our men back home.'

'People across the country were asked to build 'Victory Gardens' to help support the efforts. The country responded with over twenty million such gardens. Even though we had plenty of gas in the U.S. it was rationed to only three gallons a week so we could preserve the rubber shortage we did have. Rationing became a way of life.'

'St. Ann's Orphanage also became part of the war effort. High praise goes to the hard work and dedication the children and staff at St. Ann's Orphanage put in over the past years to support our soldiers.'

'I remember a group of us sewing together small mattresses the soldiers would carry atop their backpacks. Usually the seamstresses, dressmakers, nuns and older girls did this kind of work but there was so many to do that a group of us boys got a firsthand look at homemaking 101. Eventually, we wound up being stuck by the needles and dripping blood everywhere. This was one time we didn't complain. Some of the kids at St. Ann's had family overseas. Some dads didn't come home. We were all awarded an orange for a job well done.'

The Announcer: 'Now a word from our sponsors.'

BEECH-NUT Chewing Gum: (Sung to 10 Little Indians)
– There's four. little eight, little twelve, little Beechees
– Pure, little sweet, little fresh, little Beechees
– Twelve little flavorful Beech-Nut Beechees
– All for your enjoyment

– The candy coated gum that everyone favors
– Take your choice of any three flavors
– Peppermint, spearmint, pepsin Beechees
– Ask for Beech-Nut Beechees

The announcer returns: 'Now back to Marcel Marsole.'

'Thanks Mr. Announcer. I think this would be a good time to show the flip side of the coin. We, as children of the orphanage, talk about our lives in what we think is a horrible place. Of course we do! We are children torn from our families. But what about

90

these nuns who have dedicated their lives to try to make things a little bit better for us. We tend to look upon them as monsters who hated us. Just listen to the stories we have told. But in reality, they are no different than any other person who walks this earth. Some are good, some bad, and some are just indifferent.'

'I think this is a good time to be fair to our counterparts. The nuns of St. Ann's Orphanage had a job to and I believe they did it well. Let me read this article to you without interruption. In 1942, at the time of the pool dedication one nun was quoted saying.'

"There will always be orphans in war and in peace and we must take care of them. Some mothers feel burdened when they must care for three or four children. There are 224 children, many of them orphaned, at St. Anne's. The number of children has increased materially during the last few months. At present the house is nearly filled to capacity. To feed those youngsters requires 816 loaves of bread each week. Fifty gallons of milk are required for one day. Sixteen pounds of butter are consumed each day."

"As yet, sugar is still plentiful and though the children use it carefully, they eat 300 pounds each week, which will be about their allotment when rationing begins. St. Anne's is health conscious and nutrition is the rule. Cod liver oil is used by the barrel. The smallest children take it readily and about three gallons are licked down each week. These items are in addition to fruit, cereals, and all the other supplies necessary for well-rounded and varied meals."

"The staff, sisters and older children must work together to prepare and serve meals, make or make over clothes for children, buy shoes, see that the children get to school, that they have their daily naps when they are small, and plenty of sleep for all, as well as play time and snack times."

Marcel continued. 'What I see in this article is a cooperation of all members of the orphanage, including the children. Earlier articles portrayed the nuns as the sole support and providers to the children. A big change is underway as to how an orphanage is perceived by all.'

'Well, Marcel, it seems we all see things in different ways and have our own opinions as such. Some days were terrible, others were just bearable. But all in all, I guess it wasn't all bad.'

'Chip, everyone looks at their situation in a different way. Take what you experienced and make something good of it. Remember to just let it go. Otherwise, you will have a miserable life. As for my guests, it is time to conclude our show for tonight. Ivan A. Bandon and I, Marcel Marsole, bid you all a safe and happy journey through life. Goodnight.'

We all said goodbye as the announcer started talking. 'Here is the latest news update: Dateline: September 2, 1945: It is official. WWII has finally come to an end. The U.S. has declared this day as VJ Day or Victory over Japan Day. Just moments ago the Japanese officially surrendered aboard the USS Missouri. On June 6th a new kind of bomb, an atomic bomb, was dropped over Hiroshima, Japan instantly killing nearly 80,000 Japanese citizens. On June 9th another 40.000 people were killed when a second atomic bomb was dropped over Nagasaki. These bombings and the intervention of Russia finally convinced the Emperor of Japan to lay down his sword.'

Upon these final words the radio went silent. I said. "Wow, what a way to end a broadcast. Just think of how many people in our time still have stories about WWII. Incredible!"

A figure appeared from the end of the room. "Bonjour mes amis. I am Donald. I apologize for my tardiness. I have been asked to take you on a tour of our grounds here at St. Ann's Orphanage. Would you mind following me?" With his request, we got up from our comfortable chairs and followed Donald to the rear of the room, out a door onto a covered porch and down two flights of stairs to ground level.

A 1940'S WALK ABOUT

To our surprise daylight was upon us. Even though we were cast in the sun's shadow by the building, we could tell the sun shone brightly. We gazed upon that beautiful view before us of the Worcester landscape. How could we ever forget it? Past the playground area we could see the sprawling farm lands. It was definitely midsummer as the crops were near full growth, ready for gathering their gifts of nature. Donald guided us to the south of the building where we then turned toward the east and walked up the incline towards the main building. We had to cover our eyes as the sun appeared over the building.

"As you can see, the repairs to the building are now complete. The December 27, 1939 fire started there in the first floor rubbish shoot and quickly spread up the shaft to the roof and mushroomed out onto the fourth floor. The damage to the building was confined to this end near the side porches. It was decided to repair all that the fire had damaged as well as making other necessary repairs about the building. They completed the makeover by repainting the entire structure from the previously white hue to this dark New England color."

"It really makes it look so new." Said Christine. "I guess a bad thing can turn out to be a good thing in the long term, can't it?" "Look there," I said. "There is that infamous covered bridge that goes between the two buildings. Whoever thought of that should have a plaque in his or her name placed upon it. Just think about marching back and forth between those two buildings many times a day in a snow storm or freezing temperatures. Back then we just took it for granted."

Donald continued walking around the south side of the building. "As you can see the barn and stables are in full working order. The hired hands keep pretty busy during these times. Extra gardens have been planted for the war effort. They call them Victory Gardens. In the fall, half the canned goods we produce will be shipped off to our men overseas along with all the clothing and bed mats our fine ladies of the house have prepared."

"There are our quarters. These two old buildings have been around since before the orphanage was here. I believe this was the farmer's house and his hired hands used the other one. Now, that one is for the hired men and the other is for the hired women. Each end of the house has a chimney flue with a fireplace on each floor. There are plenty of trees on the farm to supply the fireplaces. The men cut, gather, split and stack the logs between the two houses for easy access. The ladies have to collect the wood from the stacks themselves since the men are not allowed into their house unless repairs are required."

"I guess we didn't realize that the orphanage is really a big business enterprise." Said Rosalie. "When you think about it you can see how important every aspect must be handled. I worked at a college campus housing department and understand the logistics of it all. The nuns in charge also have to make sure the entire farm is in proper working order and running smooth each and every day. Kudos to the Grey Nuns for pulling it off all those years."

"Come," said Donald. "Our prize possession awaits us." As we walked along the side of the building approaching Granite Street, we saw it, the Grotto of St. Ann's Orphanage in all its glory. The sun seemed to create a halo above the stone shrine. What a sight to behold! Shivers ran up our spines. Memories flooded into our hearts and minds. Who could ever forget this magnificent site?

"For the 1941 Golden Anniversary of St. Ann's Orphanage, L'Ami des Orphelins Society, namely The Friends of Orphans Society, gifted the 'Grotto of Our Lady of Lourdes and St. Bernadette'." I added. "You know Donald, buy the 1960s this grotto will be considered one of the most beautiful Lourdes' shrines in New England. This place will be a popular devotional center for Worcester Catholics. Unfortunately, all good things will come to an end and time will take its toll on this place."

"Yes," said Rosalie. "But, for those years it will be a grand place. Many devotions were carried out along this hillside. Children were photographed here after receiving their First Communion, Graduates of St. Ann's paid their last respects here. New entrants to St. Ann's found solstice in praying at this site. Many wishes were requested here. I really believe that most of them were granted."

"Come along." Said Donald. "Let us walk along Granite Street to the other end of the building. As you can see the buildings blend together so well. The new facade makes you think these old buildings could last another fifty years. We can only hope." As we make it around the front of the huge structure we saw a sidewalk connected to a circular walk surrounding a large pool.

"Here we are. the best toy of all for everyone here at St. Ann's. On March 29, 1942 this grand pool was presented by the Harmony Club. They were another benefactor that helped us by raising funds for the orphanage. The pool is set on a plot 350 by 200 feet. As you can see the land is beautifully landscaped and shrubbery aligns the walkway. It cost more than $6,000. At the deepest point, the pool is four feet. A cement walk, eight feet wide surrounds the pool, on which the children can roller skate when there is no swimming."

"Oh Donald," I said. "We could tell you stories about this place." "Joe." blurted Rosalie. "Tell him the one about the Baby Ruth." "You have to remember Rosie, this is 1942 and none of that has happened yet. We can't let the cat out of the bag."

"It is alright Mr. Joe. You must remember I am like you. We are all here in spirit only. I know what you know. My fellow spirits and I are here to enlighten your hearts and souls to St. Ann's past and how the children coped with what they had no control of. Let us continue our walk to the auditorium. This is a special place where you can bear witness to what I speak."

Off we went, walking down the north side path to the brick dormitory building. We of course viewed the crossover bridge to the right of us before entering the building. It still amazed us. Once in the hallway we walked to a doorway on the right and turned in to see the middle section of the large auditorium.

Donald spoke once more. "It seems that the 1940s would be the grand debut of entertainment at St. Ann's Orphanage. With the remarkable entry of movies, especially that of Walt Disney, entertainment became a staple in the lives of many children here. The big start happened to coincide with the Golden Jubilee. Plans made for that weeklong celebration had to include entertaining the thousand guests who would be visiting. Who better to impress these crowds? The children, of course!"

"So a year of selecting songs, dances and plays was underway. Selecting the right child for an acting part or a singing position and matching boy and girl dancing partners was crucial in getting everything right. Rehearsals were held day after day. And let's not forget the costumes! The dressmakers, seamstresses, nuns and the older girls all had to create and make those beautiful outfits for every single child on the stage. The boys and men didn't sit by idly either. They had the task of creating and building those magnificent scenes required for the stage."

"This became a win-win enterprise for the children and the orphanage. The crowds loved the performances. The children loved performing and doing something special for others. It made their time at St. Ann's more meaningful and tolerable. It would also become a great way to bring in donations to the orphanage. Doing special performances was also another way to say thank you or to give tribute to their benefactors."

"A good example of that was in 1947 when L'Ami des Orphelins Society, namely The Friends of Orphans Society, celebrated their 25th Anniversary with a banquet at St. Ann's Orphanage. It was a one day, gala event that was capped off with the grand entertainment of the children."

"My friends, I beg your leave. It is now time for me to depart. I will leave you in the good hands of a learned couple who will provide you with other stories from this decade. I believe you will enjoy this segment of your journey. Here they are now, Rose Aimee and Gilbert."

Chapter 7

The New World Order

TRANSITION INTO THE NEW WORLD ORDER

After introductions Donald departed and we witnessed the transformation of the auditorium into a beautiful banquet setting. We were escorted to a large table set up in front of the stage. It appeared that we would be the guests of honor for this gala event. As we sat in our designated seats we saw two rows of tables. A group of boys and girls marched into the auditorium and the boys took their seats in the row to our right and the girls to the left.

Rosalie said. "This is getting interesting." Rose Aimee smiled. "This banquet is going to be a little bit different than the other banquets held here. Think of it this way, you are really not here in the eyes these children. Yet, they do see someone in your seats. To them you are reporters from the Worcester Telegram, and Times Free Press doing an article on the children's stories at St. Ann's Orphanage."

Christine interjected. "Now, this scenario really does sound interesting, and confusing. But I'll bite." I said. "I see. This way we can actually talk with the children and hear stories from them. Right?" "Oui, Mr. Joe." replied Gilbert. "There are no nuns or staff from the orphanage here, so the children can speak freely with anonymity." "Well then," I said. "I have certainly got an appetite from all these decades of travel. So let's get on with the feast."

With that, Gilbert took himself to the podium set up in the middle of our table. "Good afternoon. I thank you all for coming to this unprecedented event. I am Gilbert Gamache, your emcee and moderator today. Today's format will be simple enough. Each child here will be given the opportunity to tell us a story they were part of here at St. Ann's Orphanage. Our guest reporters will also have the chance to talk with you as we go along. All we ask is that each of you be as truthful as possible in your recollections."

"Let me introduce you to our guests. To my far right is Theresa Marie from the Worcester Telegram. You may refer to her as Ms. Terry. Secondly, we have Nina Christine from the Times Free Press. You may refer to her as Ms. Nina. To my left is Joseph Bernier from the Worcester Gazette. Mr. Joe to you. Finally, we have Rose Aimee Bernier who is my special assistant and guest commentator. If you would kindly look in front of you, you will find a large card with a name printed upon it. Instead of using your real names, we will use these names to communicate with each of you. Rose Aimee will now begin with a short commentary."

With that Rose Aimee traded places with Gilbert at the podium. "The 1940s was quite a decade. Constant changes were witnessed throughout the years. It started out with a major war brewing overseas with our eminent entry. Children entering St. Ann's came at a time where total control and discipline were a must in the minds of those in charge. As the decade progressed and the war came to fruition an unspoken bond was created between the staff and the children. You were no longer seen as a group that needed continuous punishment. It became discipline as needed. At least, up to a point. Today, your stories and recollections will

100

hopefully validate this notion. With this in mind I would like to open the floor to anyone who would like to tell a story or ask a question."

Everyone was a bit apprehensive to begin with, so Ms. Nina broke the ice. "Is it true that the Worcester Gazette started the tradition of collecting and bringing Christmas gifts for all the children, which included a visit from Santa Claus? Let's see, Miss Laura. How long have you been here?"

Caught by surprise Laura, a bit shaken, regained her composure and spoke. "Bonjour, I have lived here for four years. At all those Christmas parties I do remember Santa visiting us. It was a wonderful time. We all gathered here, in the auditorium, just before he arrived. The younger children were so excited. He went up on stage and showed us magic tricks before calling each of us, by name, to come up and receive a special gift from him."

"Thank you Miss Laura." said Ms. Nina. "It has been publicized and pictured in the paper for many years showing the Worcester Gazette Santa visiting St. Ann's Orphanage. He has handed out thousands of gifts over the years along with entertaining the children with his magic acts. The most wonderful part of all was how you children reciprocated by singing carols, dancing and performing the Nativity. It sure was fun for everyone who attended."

A hand was seen being raised from the boys table. "Hello," called out Edmond. "I remember my first Christmas here. I was invited to spend the holiday in the home of this wonderful family from the north side of Worcester. They were so nice to me and my little sister. We really had a great time. I guess they liked us too, because we have been staying with them during the holidays and summer vacations for the past three years. They will always be in our hearts and thoughts for as long as we live."

"Well said, Edmond." Was Mr. Joe's reply. "It is amazing to see how many Worcester families opened their doors to you children during the holidays and summer vacations. I'm sure many fond memories were made during these times. Like the visit from Santa, this too became a long lasting tradition of St. Ann's Orphanage."

Gilbert spoke. "So that we all get a chance to tell a story, we will start on our left, then right, in a girl-boy manner. So, that would make it Janette's turn to tell her story to us. Janette."

"I would like to thank all of you for giving us a chance to tell our stories. Mine is a sad one. I came here early in this decade and found this place to be uncaring of my situation. My family was very religious, going to church and being at all of their functions. My sisters and I would always say our prayers and obey all the teachings of the church. When my mom got sick our parish priest did not console us. He didn't provide us any help other than telling my father to send us to this orphanage."

"My sisters and I were never punished at home. There was no need. But, when we arrived here we were immediately reprimanded for just being sad! The nuns told us that sort of behavior would not be tolerated. We were told to get over it! Our parents had left us here and we were now under their charge. While living here we were always praying for forgiveness. Yet we felt we had nothing to be forgiven for. We did nothing wrong!"

"My faith was being destroyed bit by bit every day I lived here. By the time my sisters and I left we were completely distraught. We felt that God had abandoned us. Trust in our religion was gone. I just pray that someday someone will show me the true meaning to all of this. Thank you for listening,"

"Thank you so much for sharing such a touchy subject, Janette." Said Rose Aimee. "This is exactly what we are here for. The early days of the 1940s was a very difficult time. Some took the discipline harder than others. A lot of it came from the particular situation that brought you children here. Most people didn't understand how an organization like an orphanage could incorporate such rules. Next story will come from Roger."

"Thank you Ms. Rose Aimee. Discipline is what my story is about. As we all know, war was looming during the early 40s. A group of us boys made an effort to prepare ourselves for what we all knew would eventually happen. That is, the United States would go to war and we would soon become of age to enlist and fight for our country. With our group established and in uniform we went and became part of a three-day program that was held by the American Legion, Canadian, Scandinavian and Swedish clubs for the Worcester Canteen Fund. On September 7, 1942 my group did St. Ann's Orphanage proud by performing military style drills with rifles and flags. The exercises brought loud cheers from the crowd. We can only hope that we will soon hear victory cheers."

Ms. Terry replied. "Thank you Roger. I have seen some photos of the drill team. Very impressive looking group of young men to say the least. Julia, I believe you have the floor."

"Yes. Thank you. I have some enjoyable recollections of the pool I'd like to share. As we all know, the pool was dedicated on March 29, 1942. That summer was the best summer ever at St. Ann's. Besides giving us something to enjoy it also gave us time to forget our problems, at least for that moment. It was also a real test of the nuns' character. I mean, just think of having a large group of girls and boys scantly clothed all splashing about, enjoying themselves. It makes me chuckle just thinking about it. Remember, modesty was their top priority when we took showers. They made us wear those goofy looking outfits. Even the boys had to wear some kind of bathing pants."

"Now, here we were splashing about in this coed setting. Boys and girls virtually bathing TOGETHER! 'Heaven strike me down.' I heard one of the sisters cry out. They tried to keep us apart but that was fruitless. Eventually, reason took over their resolve and acceptance prevailed. I guess it came to them that they didn't need to yell at us from the poolside. All they needed to do was give us that 'look' and we would freeze with fear."

"Roller skating was also fun during the summertime. The eight-foot-wide cement walkway around the pool provided us with a nice smooth path. As much as we enjoyed the summertime swims and roller skating about the pool it also provided us with winter sports. Ice skating was certainly a big challenge for us. It was so funny to see us take so long to put on those skates, only to end up constantly falling on our behinds. I don't know why ice skates aren't made the same way as roller skates. With two rows of wheels I could stand up on the roller skates. But ice skates with only one blade, impossible."

"On occasion we had real figure skaters come and perform for us. Boy, could they spin and jump. They made it look so easy. We did have so much fun. I do remember the sledding, too. We had the perfect rolling hills to sled on. I will always cherish these moments of my stay."

"Thank you Julia." Responded Ms. Nina. "I'm sure that keeping active in the winter was very important. Staying inside all day would have been quite boring. Roland, I believe it is now your turn."

"Oh yes. It is an honor to speak with you today. During last summer some of the younger kids got a chance to ride ponies that were brought here especially for them. Most of these youngsters had never been on a horse or pony. I was one of the older boys who helped the little kids up on the pony and then took them for a walk around the barn area. It was the first time I had seen some of these kids smile."

"Later that summer we couldn't believe our eyes when the Budweiser Wagon with its full complement of Clydesdales came here to visit us. To the enjoyment of the children, we all had the chance to get up close to the Clydesdales and pet them. We were all in awe at the enormous size of the horses. They even allowed us to climb aboard the wagon. Mollie, their Dalmatian, was so friendly to us. She was so happy to see us. She wagged her tail so fast and couldn't stop licking our faces. We talked about that day the rest of the summer."

"Merci, Roland." Said Rose Aimee. "Beatrice, you are next."

"Merci, thank you Ms. Rose Aimee. Speaking French is easier than you think. At least for youngsters. A lot of people forget that many French Canadians migrated into northern New England. There were many communities that had a large population of French speaking people. You could almost see the path from Worcester, up through Fitchburg and into southern New Hampshire where a great many families settled. Many descendants still live within the triangle of Nashua, Keene and Manchester."

"Names like Bernier, Belanger, Gamache, Deschenes and Lizotte, are just a few of the families that settled in the area. My great uncle Joseph Bernier was a famous explorer of the Hudson Bay and helped Canada gain sovereignty over much of the arctic territories. You can read all about his historic explorations."

"With a large French community in the Worcester area and an abundance of children needing care St. Ann's French Canadian Orphanage became an integral part of the community. With the arrival of the Grey Nuns, from Montreal, it was self-evident this would be a French speaking institution."

"In the early days it was not a problem since everyone spoke French. But, as the years passed children from the non-French sectors of Worcester also needed asylum. It became more of an issue. It was imperative that the children quickly learn

French. English would be the second language here with only classroom study. The saying goes, 'Children have brains like sponges' was proven true as the young children did learn the French language quickly, both as a requirement and a necessity. We were spoken to only in French. So French had to be our response. Somehow we were much more resilient than we thought and we did survive the undertaking."

"Beatrice," said Mr. Joe. "your history lesson was very interesting. I am sure many of our readers would not even have thought about how important the French and English languages were to the structure of the orphanage. I see, it is now time to hear from Napoleon."

"With the war at its end many stories were coming back to our shores. One in particular hit close to home. Many remember that during the war we were told about the tragic story of the five Sullivan brothers that died side by side on board their ship when it was attacked by the enemy. Well, today I have happier news. Lucien & Julien, brothers in arms and brothers at home have made it back from the war safe and sound. What is so amazing is that they both were on the beaches of Normandy, France on D-Day. Neither knew they were just a short distance apart from each other surviving the barrage of enemy fire. They not only survived the beaches but also the bloody trek across France. Now, after their long encounter with the enemy they have arrived back to the good old U.S. of A. Tomorrow, the local townspeople are giving them a hero's welcome."

"You may ask why I brought this up as it doesn't have anything to do with St. Ann's Orphanage. But indeed it does. Lucien is the father of my two sweet cousins and Julien is my father. Now that they are safely home we can leave the orphanage and return home. We are only a few of the lucky ones that have this chance. My prayers were answered. I will forgive my captors and think only fondly of this place as a means to an end. After today's meeting with you, my cousins and I will gather the few things we came with and go home. We will pray for all the new friends we have made."

Wiping a tear from her eye, Rose Aimee replied with all sincerity. "Merci, thank you Napoleon for such a heartwarming story. We all wish you and your families the best that life has to offer." Rose Aimee turned to the audience and called out to Isabelle.

"Good afternoon. According to my card, I am Isabelle. I too, like Napoleon, want to look back at my time here as a fond memory. So, I would like to express the happiness of being a child in such a beautiful location. I enjoyed playing with so many girls that were my age. Making friends was wonderful and also sad. Even though we knew that at any moment one of us could leave we looked at it as a good thing. We just wished the nuns would have let us say goodbye."

"I loved playing in the fields and play areas. We would take nature walks around the farm and comment on the beauty of the landscape high above Worcester. The nuns had us prepare a picnic basket and we would go across Granite Street on the other side of the Grotto and have a wonderful time discussing girl stuff. One time a group of boys and girls went on an outing to Green Hill Park. That was an enjoyable afternoon."

"Around the grounds of St. Ann's are gardens and trees of all kinds. There are even grape vines that produce some deliciously sweet, dark purple grapes in late summer. Blueberry picking was a fun thing to do. I think we ate more than what ended up in our pails. We did make good use of the grounds."

"We played baseball together. That is, the boys, girls and get this, even the nuns. Oh yah. They were pretty good, too. They taught us how to catch and throw and hit the ball. We had lots of fun and a few good laughs was had by all."

"Thank you Isabelle." Said Ms. Terry. "I can just picture the excitement of the game. It looks like we have reached our last story teller. My sources at the newspaper tell me that you are the young man with many stories to tell. So, without further ado, I give the floor to Royal."

"Hello, my name is Royal. I was just a babe in '41 so I don't remember much about that time. I entered St. Ann's when I was six. With most of our soldiers back home from the war it was becoming just a bad memory and 'Reconstruction' was the new word. Like most boys, I was moved to a boys' home across town when I was 12. You could say I was part of the transition. Before telling you a short story let me add to some of the other stories you have heard."

"Each year, just before Christmas, you were asked to pick three presents you would like to get. At the Christmas party you would get just one of your choices. You were allowed to play with this gift until the holidays were over. Like it or not, after that they became community property."

"I guess I was the right age for most of the things going on here. There was this new nun who was quite different than most of the other nuns. Over the years she helped improve our lives in different ways. She started a 'Good Points' program that allowed us to collect points whenever we did something good. The more points you got the better chance you had to go on special outings and such. I enjoyed going to the movies and getting a Charleston Chew for my movie snack."

"At one point this nun actually got permission to change over one of the cloak rooms in the old building into a hobby room. We got a special visit from Bishop Wright and Father Alfred because of it. We made all kinds of things. One time we made airplane models, mine was a PS1 Mustang. The dining room was upstairs from our hobby room. The round tables in the dining room were just big enough to have four small chairs about them. We were given permission to hang our models from the ceilings above them. I bet you they'll still be there ten years from now."

"The description of the showers someone earlier described is correct. In the basement of the dormitory were two shower rooms. One on the girls' side and the other on the boys' side. The boys had to wear these silly looking bloomers. Boy that was completely embarrassing. And yes, there was a special belt one of the nuns liked to use that would hurt like the dickens but did not leave the usual welts. You always stayed fearful of repercussions so you did your best to behave at all times. It was better to get those 'Good Points' than to be wacked."

"Wetting your bed was no picnic either. If you didn't find a way to sneak under the beds to the toilet without getting caught and you peed your bed, no good points were going to save you. I've heard different tales of kids having to sleep in it and others having their noses rubbed in it. I even heard of the nuns making you go to every kid and tell them what you did. Fortunately, I was a 'dry' sleeper."

"The kids did have numbers. Mine was #72 and my cousin's was #82. We had side by side bins in, what we called, the cubby closet. Our clothes were also inscribed with our number."

"There was also a 'Big Brother' program. This gave us boys a chance to talk to an older male and ask questions about what was happening with our body changes. Obviously, the nuns hadn't a clue. Our Big Brothers would take us out to some of the local hangouts around Worcester. The local fun parks were also on the list of places to go."

"There have been stories of kids sneaking or running away from St. Ann's. There was this boy who told me he and his friend decided to go visit an aunt who lived a few towns away. So off they went one night. They walked down Granite Street to route 20. They thought they were doing pretty good time walking along route 20 when a bus pulled over and offered them a free ride. I guess they forgot that there is no such thing as a free ride."

"Anyway, they accepted the ride. Shortly after, they found themselves at the local police station. The next thing they knew, a nun was picking them up and bringing them back to St. Ann's Orphanage. We won't go into any further details. I think we all get the picture of what happened next."

"Why thank you Royal for your array of happenings here at St. Ann's." said Mr. Joe. "It appears we have one more tale to talk about with Miss Claire. Is it true Claire, that you have been with St. Ann's Orphanage since 1938 and have been witness to all of this for the past 12 years?"

"That is correct." Mr. Joe. "As a true orphan, I have been a part of this institution for most of my young life. I was placed here when I was four years old. Next year I will graduate from St. Ann's Orphanage and go on to Holy Cross College. I will be studying child psychology and hope to become a doctor in this field. I think my experience here will provide great benefit to my learning. Someday, I hope to support places like St. Ann's in providing a better interpretation of the children's feelings during these hard times and also an insight into their response to these situations as they get older."

Ms. Rosie spoke. "You are amazing! That is a very commendable and unselfish thing for you to do. I am sure you will help many children through their difficult times. We all wish you well in your future endeavors."

"Thank you." Ms. Rosie. "I would like to take this time to give honor to a very special lady, Doris Joyce. We all know her as Miss. Joyce. She has been an inspiration to so many children. She was hired as a dance instructor. Her dedication to her work has inspired so many of us. She took on a very big task and made it look so easy to the audiences who watched the performances."

"The children learned how to properly stand and hold their partners. Each step they perform is full of grace and composure. These performers, younglings and elders, command the audience's attention. As far as I am concerned, the performances of all the dancers is perfection at its best. Miss. Joyce is the creator of these wonderful artists. Need I say any more?"

Ms. Rosie spoke again. "I can assure you, Claire that Miss. Joyce will be at St. Ann's Orphanage for many years to come. She will continue to inspire hundreds more children while she is here. I'm sure there are many, many children who look back on their stay here with a bit of fondness because of Miss. Joyce."

Gilbert stepped back up to the podium. "I see the time has quickly passed us by, and it is time to thank our honored guests for taking the time to listen to your stories. Messengers of the children, we wish each and every one of you a safe and wonderful journey through life."

The boys and girls stood up and marched out the side entrance as we applauded them. We called out as they departed. "Thank you so much for coming here and talking with us."

Gilbert looked at us and said. "Come with me and Rose Aimee. We will take you to the TV room in the main building. There is a special show on tonight just for you." Without hesitation we followed them.

Chapter 8

The Orphan Show

ROSIE RIVET

After being escorted into the main building we were shown to the TV room. There was a group of seats for us to sit in and what looked like a brand new color TV. We turned to say goodbye to Gilbert and Rose Aimee but they had already vanished. The room did not look like a room from the orphanage. It looked more like a dressing room. Along the wall were high chairs in front of a long desk and huge mirror.

All of a sudden the television turned on. It was going crazy. The screen looked like it was trying to tune into a channel. First snow, then lines flickering this way and that. A voice emanated from the speakers.

'There is nothing wrong with your television set. Do not attempt to adjust the picture. We are controlling the transmission. You are about to enter another dimension. A dimension not only of sight and sound, but of mind. A journey into a wondrous land of memories. Next stop, the Outer Limits of the Twilight Zone!'

Christine spoke. "What in the world was that all about?"

Before anyone could respond a man and a few women came in. He spoke first. "Good evening. We must hurry and prepare ourselves. Please sit up in front of the mirrors so that your makeup ladies can take care of you. I asked. "What's going on?" "Oh, that's right, you were rushed here so quickly. Of course you don't know. You have been selected to be the guests of Joela Fountaine on the Orphan Show."

We all looked at each other with a questionable grimace before Christine muttered. "If I'm guessing correctly, you are telling us we are going to be on a TV show called the Orphan Show. Is that right?"

"You people must be joking. Everyone watches the Orphan Show. It's on every night after the news. Rosie Rivet saying; 'There's Joela Fountaine'. The band, the guests, and the audience." He shook his head a bit and wagged his arms. He could still see a confused expression on our faces. "You've got to be kidding me."

We again looked at each other before I came up with an answer. "I get it. We've just stepped into the 'Outer Limits of the Twilight Zone'. So, am I right saying that the lady on the TV is the real Rosie the Riveter?"

"Yes and No. Rosie Riveter is not just one person but a cultural icon of all the women of the World War II wartime effort in the United States. Rosie Rivet is just one of those many inspiring women who helped embody the feminist movement that launched women into the man's world."

I said. "I do understand how important she is for women's rights. The future will be better because of her efforts. So, what are we here to do?"

"You will be telling stories you have heard as well as your own to Joela Fountaine. He'll be asking you and the other guests a lot of questions. Now please, let these ladies get you presentable. In the mean time you can watch the monitors. Rosie Rivet is warming up the audience as we speak. You three will be Mr. Fountaine's first guests. I will stop back in about ten minutes to bring you to the stage."

"It looks like we're about to be TV stars." said Christine. "I wonder. Do you think something else is going to happen to us out there? We really can't be seen by the people of this time, remember?"

"That's a good point." said Rosalie. "I guess we'll just have to wait and see how the spirits are going to pull this one off."

We sat in our high chairs and let the make-up artists recreate what we already believed to be beautiful. On the monitor we watched as Rosie Rivet finished warming up the audience and moved to her seat at the end of a row of couches. Before sitting down she made her big introduction.

"Ladies and gentlemen, welcome to the Orphan Show staring Joela Fountaine. Tonight we bring you a New Year's Eve 1960 special edition of the Orphan Show. We will be taking a look back on this past decade, the 1950s with a fine tooth comb. Our guests all have one thing in common. In one way or another their lives have been affected by St. Ann's Orphanage in Worcester, Massachusetts."

"We will hear from Faith, Hope and Disparity, followed by Patty Cake, Father Brown and Sister Gray. They will provide us with some insight into the multifaceted St. Ann's Orphanage. We will also have a special appearance from our good friend from the North Pole, Santa himself. You will be entertained by our one and only Orphan Band and guest music group the Depth of Despair."

THERE'S JOELA FOUNTAINE

"So, ladies and gentlemen, let's not keep him waiting any longer. There's Jooooela Fountaine."

The band plays the Orphan Show theme song as Joela Fountaine enters center stage, finds his mark on the floor and readies himself to present his monologue. He smiles and bows a few times until the audience quiets down.

"Good evening, thanks for coming tonight. I see lots of unaccompanied boys and girls in the audience tonight. I guess your parents couldn't come. Oh, that's right! Your orphans." He chuckles but gets no response from the crowd. "Ouch, first joke and I feel like I've been left on the church doorstep."

"Well, if you think that's bad. Check out some of these beauties I've come across. I'm sure some of you may have heard them before. So please don't judge me. I am only the messenger not the writer. OK, here we go."

"What is an orphan's worst day at school? – Parent Night."
The audience sat in silence with a concerning look on their faces.

"Knock, knock. – Who's there? – Not your parents"
Rim shot from the drummer with no audience reply

"What do you call an orphan's family tree? – A stump"
The audience is getting very uncomfortable.

118

"Why do orphans go to church? - So they have someone to call father."
Some boos and hisses emanate from the upper seats.

"What do orphans get at Christmas? – Lonely"
Now you can hear hissing and booing growing louder.

"This man and his wife saw a boy dressed in rags sitting outside the grocery store.
The wife said. "You're an orphan."
The boy replied. "Yes, who gave me away?"
The man replied. "Your parents."

At this point the audience was outraged. Joela responded. "All right, all right. Don't take a hissy fit. I'm just trying to make a point here by showing you how it feels to hear these kind of jokes. You've heard that old saying, 'Sticks and stones will break my bones, but words will never hurt me.' Hah. We've all been there. I don't know about you, but none of those jokes made me feel good. This is one of many ways words do hurt you."

"It's bad enough that you have such a loss to deal with. Now you get these stupid jokes and demeaning things said to you." The crowd mumbled in agreement. "Well, tonight we will see and hear good, bad, and indifferent stories straight from the children and management of St. Ann's Orphanage."

With that the audience realized Joela was only setting the stage for what was to be a memorable New Year's Eve. They all applauded as the Orphan Show band began to play and Joela set off to sit at his desk.

FAITH, HOPE AND DISPARITY

With the commercial break complete we find Joela Fountaine sitting at his desk ready to announce his first guests. "Tonight our first guests come to us from a place beyond our imagination. I am told they have a futuristic vision beyond our scope when it comes to St. Ann's Orphanage. Ladies and gentlemen, Faith, Hope and Disparity." The audience applauses and we enter the stage. We are Faith, Hope and Disparity and are greeted with a warm handshake from Joela before proceeding to the couch set next to his desk.

"Are you comfortable?" We nodded, yes. "Great. I see you have made it easy for us, Faith, Hope and Disparity, by sitting in order, left to right. Now according to my notes, as part of the St. Ann's family, you three bring to us an overall perspective but not the demographics of the orphanage. Faith, can you help me with this?"

"Of course. During its lifetime St. Ann's Orphanage will take into its care well over ten thousand orphans and boarders. This provides an unprecedented diversity of children ethnically, physically, emotionally and spiritually. Each and every child has a unique situation. Let me give you just a few of the hundreds of different circumstances: First, a single child may have lost both parents and is truly orphaned. Second, a single child may have lost one parent. Death may come in many forms. Third, multiple siblings from one family may have come to the same fate."

"Situations are many like illnesses, abandonment and abusive homes. I could go on all evening. As I said, there are hundreds of scenarios. Each child has their own, unique story. We are here representing an overall perspective of this demographic situation."

"I see," said Joela with a confusing look. "I guess there is much to talk about. So let's get started with the heart and soul of the orphans' spirituality. Maybe you can provide us with an insight into this subject, Hope."

"Thanks, Joela. It seems religion is a major factor in the lives of the children at St. Ann's. Most of the children who come to St. Ann's are already catholic or are brought into the catholic fold during their stay. Prayers are a constant daily routine." But this story is not about what happens at the orphanage but how their faith was carried with them once they left St. Ann's."

"Faith can tell you how it was with her."

"Thanks Hope. Let me digress first. At the orphanage, the children's faith was constantly tested by the nuns and staff. Many children had a difficult time adapting to the new lifestyle they were forced into. I entered St. Ann's as a devout catholic. At age five it was all I knew. I was a bilingual child, speaking French and English. These were assets at St. Ann's."

"I adapted quickly and soon was part of the student educational TV show presented on WWOR in Worcester,

Massachusetts. My brother and I were also chosen to be part of the stage dancers and singers. We'll talk about that a little later."

"As nice as this sounds, our spirits were slowly broken. Eventually, many lost their faith. Just picture at night time a dormitory filled with fifty or so young children crying their eyes out from loneliness and fear. We were too young to understand what was going on. All we knew was our mom wasn't there to tuck us in, or kiss and hug us and whisper goodnight. There were no stories read to us so we could fall calmly to sleep."

"Let me side step for a second and tell you how I made it through these trying times. An angel came to help me and the other little girls. Yah, I know how skeptical people are about these things. But, I truly believe in my Guardian Angel. Here's what happened to me."

"There I lay in my sad excuse for a bed with my hands neatly folded on top of the blanket as required by the nuns. The ceiling was dark and there were no views out the windows for me to gaze upon the stars and moon. The tears I shed were slowly drying. I could hear Elsa next to me still weeping. She hadn't been right since she arrived at St. Ann's. Some kids really had a hard time."

"It was odd but I felt a presence nearby. I turned toward Elsa and could not believe my eyes. A small, but older girl, with long, dark hair was kneeling next to the weeping child. She was dressed in a long, dark navy dress with a large white collar. She put her arm about Elsa and softly sang '*Chut petit bébé ne pleure pas!* (Hush little baby don't you cry!)."

"I was intrigued by what I was witnessing so I leaned over and said. '*Bonsoir. Je suis Faith. Qui êtes-vous et où venez-vous?*' (Who are you and where do you come from?) She told me her name was Ruth and was eleven years old. She was an angel assigned to comfort the sad and crying children of St. Ann's Orphanage. She too had lived within these same walls nearly fifty years ago. Unfortunately, she had fallen ill and taken to the Lord at an early age."

"Ruth lived all the hardships and sadness that we were experiencing. Her singing was so peaceful and calming. From that night on, whenever I felt sad or alone I would hear her beautiful voice. She loved to sing to us the beautiful song 'Smile'. Please, watch the monitors and hear for yourselves as the infamous Nat King Cole sings for us."

The soft voice of Nat King Cole began along with a slideshow of photos from St. Ann's Orphanage. Here are the words:

Smile though your heart is aching
Smile even though it's breaking
When there are clouds in the sky, you'll get by
If you smile through your fear and sorrow
Smile and maybe tomorrow,
You'll see the sun come shining through for you
Light up your face with gladness
Hide every trace of sadness
Although a tear may be ever so near
That's the time you must keep on trying
Smile, what's the use of crying?
You'll find that life is still worthwhile
If you just smile
That's the time you must keep on trying
Smile, what's the use of crying?

You'll find that life is still worthwhile
If you just smile

After the audience finished their applause Faith continued. "I had found a friend and knew God had sent someone to look after us."

"Even with this encouraging event we were constantly given the impression that we were not deserving of God's love. We had to pray for his forgiveness. We had no idea as to why. We did nothing wrong. Some nuns told us we had fallen out of God's graces because of what happened with our parents. Talk about giving a child a guilt complex! Many children went to their graves feeling this guilt."

"I was disillusioned and felt God was not listening to me. It was no longer in my heart to pray. Yet I felt compelled to continue. The nuns constant gawking may have had something to do with that. My faith had been tested. Like many children, I left the orphanage less a catholic than when I went in."

"We went to live with our mom and her new husband. Even though her divorce had her excommunicated from the church she still believed in the catholic faith. We went through the motions of being good catholic children. But it took a long time for me to realize that Jesus had never forgotten me. I have been guided by many friends and family over the years. My battered heart has healed and my faith grows stronger every day."

Hope reentered the conversation. "Now let's look at the other side of the coin. I'm sure Disparity has a few words to say about this."

Disparity wastes no time replying. "As you can guess, I no longer have a religion I call my own. Don't even bother to ask me if I believe or not. Some of us truly hate being left in a world where you cannot even trust the religious factions you are part of. You can only listen to so many lies. Some are intentional, some are not. All-in-all we no longer trust these organizations."

"Look at what religion is doing to people. They take advantage of the poor or people like me who have become disillusioned. Some are subjected to intense brainwashing. They are told it is the fault of other religious groups. Kill them or they will kill you. 'Thou shalt not kill' is nothing but hypocrisy. They preach that it is an honor to kill in the name of your god and religion. We are the lambs who are brought to slaughter while the leaders reap the rewards."

Hope began his story. "Hope can only mean one thing. Sitting on the fence between faith and despair. My story started out the same as Faith's but takes a different turn. I went through my formative child and teen years as most children did. I entered the Navy where I would begin to face that question of faith, or consciousness."

"The number three has been significant during my life. You could start with the three signs of the cross. I was one of three children. I had three family members who looked out for me and my sisters when we were very young. That would be my mom, my uncle Marcel and my aunt Blanche. During my elementary school days three of us, Danny, Terry and I were great pals. Onward to junior high school where I was again part of a trio of pals with Ted and Dan. In the Navy there was Tony and Frank."

"Number one: Onward to the deep blue seas. I met death face to face and survived. As a radioman, it was part of my job to deliver messages to the captain up on the bridge. Our ship was traversing the North Atlantic Ocean when we encountered an enormous storm. The ship was bobbing about the sea like a cork."

"I made my way out the radio shack onto the deck, holding the captain's message in one hand and the guard rail in the other. I climbed the stairs and made my way around and onto the bridge. The captain read the message and signed it as always. As I left the bridge the heavy seas caused the ship to list at a steep angle and the heavy metal door I had hold of quickly flew open. It threw me out the bulkhead opening and onto the deck before slamming shut behind me."

"The incline of the rain drenched deck caused my footing to give way. I could not control my slide. My eyes opened wide as I caught sight of the deep dark ocean before me. Downhill I slid toward its ominous depths. As I drew closer I saw the skinny guard rail, opened my arms wide, and grabbed hold as my body flipped over it. The rail held and I climbed back to the deck. It wasn't until I made it to the radio shack that I realized the implications of what had just happened."

"Number two: A couple years later I was traveling on the back of my friend's motorcycle. I leaned toward his right ear to say he was following a bit too close when all I heard was him taking a gasping breath. The next thing I remember was floating about fifteen feet above the car in front of us. I could feel myself diving headfirst toward the pavement. Without hesitation I did a tuck and roll maneuver. The back of my helmet made contact first as I landed safely in the middle of the road. Again, it took a few minutes to understand what had just happened."

"Number three: A bunch of years had gone by. It was now my thirtieth birthday. My wife and I were raising three children. I was at work traveling between customer sites doing field service repairs on computer equipment. This particular day had me driving through Providence, Rhode Island."

"I was in the middle lane of Interstate 95 passing under a number of overhead bridges. Suddenly, an object struck my windshield. At first I thought my windshield had shattered. I realized someone had dropped an egg from a bridge overpass. I released my foot off the gas and checked the vehicles one each side of me. I turned on my wipers to no avail. I watched the vehicles behind me, turned on my right blinker and cautiously maneuvered my car to the right breakdown lane hoping not to strike a car or the wall."

"Once the car had stopped along the side of the highway I felt this incredible adrenalin rush go through my body. I spent the next few minutes waiting for it to subside. I called into work and took the rest of the day off. I spent the remainder of my birthday hugging my wife and kids."

"Other circumstances have confronted me but not with the intensity of these three. I've had many instances where people have cut me off. Once, I crossed an ice covered overpass with cars on both sides of me spinning out of control. I even watched a softball sized rock fly over the highway guardrail and strike my car."

"My point is that not once during any of these situations did I have someone whisper in my ear. Everything I did was reactive. There was no guardian angel whispering in my ear.

Therefore, I am skeptical. I don't dismiss my religion and I don't fully embrace it. So hope is my salvation."

Joela responds. "Interesting insight into how someone's religious beliefs have been affected. I would like to ask you, Disparity, how you fit into all of this."

SIBLINGS AND ADOPTION

"I guess you can say, I represent the siblings and adopted children of St. Ann's Orphanage. Some siblings did not go into the orphanage when their brother or sister did. For example, a younger or even older brother or sister was left in the care of a relative. Or a sibling at the orphanage was adopted and the other remained in the orphanage. Let's look at how these children may have felt."

"Take the siblings who don't go into an orphanage and are left behind. These children have no idea of what is going on. They only see their siblings being taken away. Will they ever see them again? Was it their fault their brother or sister was taken away from them? They ask themselves why they are being sent off to some other family member or to a different child care facility."

"These children may not have gone into an orphanage, but they too have the same fears and anxieties. They wonder where their mom and dad have gone. They ask themselves why their parents have done this to them. Many of these children go through the same fears of abandonment, loneliness and desperation as those placed in the orphanage."

"How can something as great as adoption be so terrifying? Isn't that supposed to be happy news for a child? How would you

128

like to be torn apart from your brothers and sisters and sent off to live with a strange man and woman? What makes them so great? All kinds of stories about adoptions have been told. I dare not talk about them tonight."

"When adoption happens there is a good chance you will never see your siblings again. Even if a family member decides to adopt one of the siblings it is not a guarantee they will allow close contact in the future. This sort of disruption in a family can have detrimental effects between family members. Questions arise like; Why her instead of me? They like him better than me. I guess I'm really worthless since even my relatives don't want me. You get the picture."

"When a circumstance happens that breaks a family apart, nothing good comes from it, at least not in the beginning. Each one of these children find their journey through life somewhat molded by these experiences. In reality it will be the individual child who will make the final decisions. The paths one choses will be presented and the past experience of your childhood will only be a guide to your choices. You can make all the excuses you want, but in the long run it will still be your choice."

Joela Fountaine. "We will continue these amazing talks with our trio. But first, I would like to introduce you to a new and upcoming group. These youngsters got their start by dancing and singing at orphanages in the surrounding area. After studying music at local colleges they started a band. Ladies and gentlemen, I present to you, Depth of Despair."

The side stage curtains open as the audience applauses. The band sings the following song to the music of the 'Kinks' – Tired of waiting (for you)

I'm So lonely
Lonely and frightened
Lonely and frightened of yoooou

So lonely
Lonely and frightened
Lonely and frightened of yoooou

I was a happy child
I lost my family and was placed with you
Then you treated me poorly
You didn't love me
What could I do?

It's my life
And I need to survive
I need to decide
On how to keep myself going
Dancing and singing
Keeping from becoming blue

'Cause I'm so lonely
Lonely and frightened
Lonely and frightened of yoooou
Of yoooooou

(Second verse, same as the first.) Songs were pretty simple in the 50s and 60s.

Upon the completion of their song and audience applause Joela Fountaine says. "Thank you gentlemen. We look forward to hearing more songs in the future. It's good when a band performs their music to the evening's theme. Now back to our trio. Faith, Hope and Disparity have much more for us this evening. So don't go away. Our other guests will help to shed light on some of the issues that have come up over these past years."

DANCING AROUND THE POLE

"We would like to hear a story or two about the new things that happened at St. Ann's Orphanage. Faith, I see you are excited to say something."

A photo of a Grotto showing Mary looking down upon a small, kneeling figure of St. Bernadette is displayed on the monitors for the audience to see.

"Oh yes. This was more of an event than a story but well worth the mention. Every May 31st the crowning of Mary was a grand event held at the Grotto of Our Lady of Lourdes across Granite Street from St. Ann's Orphanage. This was a tribute to Mary becoming crowned Queen of Heaven. Any good Catholic would know that this is the fifth glorious mystery of the rosary. The pope sanctioned the belief in Mary as Queen of Heaven in October of 1954 which made it more special."

"The procession began at St. Ann's chapel and ended up at the grotto, where embedded into the hillside were the words 'Ave Maria Immaculata' or Hail to the Immaculate Mary. It was a sight to behold. The photo on your monitors doesn't do it justice. It lacks the emotion and majestic air that could only be experienced as a participant or witness to the event. I was part of this procession in both 1954 and 1955 as one of the maypole girls."

"What a sight to behold. Some of the older girls were dressed up as angels. Older boys escorted them in their altar boy garments, depicting cherubs. As they made their way up the steps to the shrine another group of older girls followed. Boys neatly suited in a white shirt and matching pant and jacket escorted them. The girls were dressed in long white gowns with flowered wreathes adorning their heads. They all gathered around the kneeling statue of St. Bernadette who was also adorned in a flowered halo. They represented all the saints preparing the way for all the honored guests at the gates of heaven."

"There were two groups of pole bearers carrying banners in reverence to the occasion. Older boys carried large banners while the younger boys managed the smaller ones. Each group settled atop the hillside, one to the north side and one to the south side of the monument. They represented the pageantry that greeted all those walking the spiritual path to the gates of heaven."

"The maypole girls were made up of a youngling group and an elder group. They wore white dresses with matching shoes and socks. One handled the pole, suitable for her size, while a number of other girls held onto one of the long white ribbons attached to the top of the pole. They made their way to the north side of the shrine where they would perform a maypole dance during the ceremony. They represented the clouds that surrounded and guided one's journey to heaven's gate."

"The procession continued with the nuns taking charge of the remaining group of children. The girls looked so adorable in their white dresses and garland headwear. The boys were so dashing wearing their made to order suits. They took up positions on both sides of the walkway leading to the shrine in anticipation of Father Alfred's arrival. They would be the witnesses to this biblical event."

"The final group in the procession had Father Alfred surrounded by his altar boys accompanying him as he made his way up the stairs and into the grotto. This depiction would be none other than Jesus Christ surrounded by his cherubs, attending to and protecting him as he made his way through the clouds, past the bannered pageantry and through the gates of heaven."

"As the entourage made its way up the stairs a hymn was sung by the entire gathering. The girls performed their maypole dance, guiding the holy father and his attendants through heaven's gate. Once Father Alfred had settled himself at the altar the ceremony commenced with prayer. He turned to us, then back towards Mary speaking Latin words most of us could not understand. Another Hymn was sung, then another prayer."

"It was time for the crowning. Father Alfred completed another round of Latin. The crowd took to their knees. Father Alfred raised his arms high toward Mary, presenting her with an absolutely stunning wreath of flowers interlaced with gold and silver ribbons. He finished with more Latin verbiage. He turned to the crowd and gave the sign of the cross. We, in response, made the sign unto ourselves."

"The altar boys rose and assisted Father Alfred as he began his decent from the grotto. The angels and cherubs followed. The young children with their nuns in their control followed suit. The maypole dancers and the banner bearers completed the procession as they returned, across Granite Street, to the chapel for one last prayer."

The audience applauded. With the visual effects dissipating from their minds Joela spoke. "Boy, I felt as if I were there experiencing the whole thing. Well put, Faith."

Hope concluded. "The grotto is a wonderful place. It has been and will be the place to go to kneel and pray, whenever you feel inclined to do so. Please, whenever you visit Worcester, Massachusetts please stop by this spiritual landmark and say a little prayer for all the children of St. Ann's past and future."

IT IS TIME TO CONFESS OUR SINS

"So Hope," asked Joela, "Is there any religious happenings at St. Ann's Orphanage you'd like to mention?"

"Sure. First Communion was a young Catholic's first reception of the sacrament of the Holy Eucharist. When you past your seventh birthday you had to prepare yourself for this once in a lifetime event. This is one of the seven sacraments a catholic could receive. The first sacrament you would receive is Baptism. Before receiving your first communion you had to perform the sacrament of penance, or confession. Your first confession usually occurred on the day of your first communion, just hours before the ceremony."

"It would be another trying time for the children. First we had to wait in the pews for our turn to confess our sins to Father Alfred or the visiting bishop. Remember that night you didn't keep your hands on top of the blanket? Did you really have to tell him the horrible thoughts you had about Sister Vicieux? Was he keeping notes so he could tell the nuns? What if you didn't have any sins? Do you make something up so you could do the penance? Oh my, I had to say the Hail Mary five times and the Act of Contrition twice. I guess I wasn't too bad. At least not this time."

"There were many procedures to follow and new prayers to memorize. We practiced for when the priest came to you at the altar. You had to tilt your head back, open your mouth wide and produce your tongue in order to collect the holy wafer that the father placed upon it. Not too far out or too pointy. Make sure he had a good target. Whatever you do, don't let it drop! And under no circumstances do you ever, ever touch the Host! That is the body of Christ!"

"Once you made it past this life changing event you could join all the other Catholics who, in confessing their sins, saying a few prayers as penance and being forgiven for all their past indiscretions could be welcomed into the kingdom of heaven. Really?"

"But first, as a gift for your first communion, you are given a prayer book and a scapular. Usually, a scapular is a long apron like garment the nuns and priests wear. But they have been adapted over the past centuries to suit special occasions. You are given a small piece of felt with a long ribbon attached so you could wear it around your neck. A cloth picture of the Virgin Mary was sown onto this piece of felt. The nuns said you had to wear this all the time. Obviously, wear and tear, and water and sweat took its toll and it would eventually be relegated to the inside of your prayer book."

"The sacrament of Confirmation came next. When you became a teenager you were confirmed as a member of God's army. At least that's what we were told. But in reality confirmation is the strengthening of your baptism. Whereas, a priest may have presided over your baptism pouring holy water over you, a bishop would preside over your confirmation blessing you with chrism, or holy oil. The grace given in baptism is deepened and strengthened with confirmation."

"There were not many boys attending this ceremony. St. Ann's didn't retain boys over the age of puberty. That would be detrimental to peace and harmony at the orphanage. Twelve year olds were transferred to other boys' facilities or back into their family homes. Therefore, this ritual had less grandeur and was less publicized."

Disparity, who had been sitting so quietly, made his presence known. "Do you know how many times I've been condemned to hell? It all starts when you are born, 'down you go'. A good baptism took care of that. Not saying your prayers, 'down you go'. Oh my, I remember one night I was so tired that I didn't say mine. Sure enough, I woke up in the middle of the night scared

136

to death. The devil had found a way up the well at my Pepere's farm. He had a big grin on his face and was spewing fire and brimstone. He was coming after me. You bet I jumped out of my bed and said double the prayers."

"If you skipped going to church on Sundays or any of the other required masses, 'down you go'. Fish, fish Friday fish. Don't you dare eat meat on Fridays or 'down you go'. Don't you dare think bad thoughts about someone or 'down you go'. Don't think about those pretty girls with those pretty curls or 'down you go'. Oh my God! Oops, 'down I go'.

The crowd laughed and clapped in response to Disparity's bit of humor.

SIDE BY SIDE

Hope makes a request to Joela. "We'd like to finish up by performing a fairy tale story we've talked about for so many years. It starts out with two new participants, Faith and Hope, about to try out for positions in the stage dance and singing routines. Our dance instructor, Miss Joyce and music teacher Mr. Galipeau are about to see how well the new recruits can sing and dance."

With everyone's approval we got up from our couch seats and headed for the side stage. On the stage were children dressed in ragged clothing. Their hair was all a mess and they were covered with dirt and soot. To one side were the two instructors sitting in chairs with clipboards in hand. We disappeared for a moment behind the side curtain before entering from stage left (that's the right side from the audience's view). We were magically transformed to our former selves as five and six year olds. Our clothing was also in a tattered state as we walked on stage arm in arm past a street vendor.

"Bonjour, garçon. Would you like to buy an ice cream for your pretty lady?" Hope releases Faith's arm and reaches into his pockets. He pulls them inside out showing nothing but holes. He gives a big grin, shrugs his shoulders and the music begins.

Taking hold of each other's hand Faith and Hope begin a soft shoe dance to the music of 'Side-by-Side'. Hope says. "See that sun in the morning, peeking over the hill? I'll bet you're sure it always has and always will." Faith puts on a big smile and nods in agreement as we dance about the stage.

Hope sings.
"Oh, we don't have a barrel of money.
Maybe we're ragged and funny.
But, we'll travel along, singing a song, side by side.
Don't know what's coming tomorrow.
Maybe it's trouble and sorrow.
But, we'll travel the road, sharing our load, side by side."

Faith continues the song.
"Through all kinds of weather.
What if the sky should fall?
Just as long as we're together,
It doesn't matter at all.
When they've all had their quarrels and parted,
We'll be the same as we started.
Just a-travelling along, singing a song, side by side."

We both sing in harmony.
"Oh, we don't have a barrel of money.
Maybe we're ragged and funny.
But, we'll travel along, singing a song, side by side.

138

Don't know what's coming tomorrow.
Maybe it's trouble and sorrow.
But, we'll travel the road, sharing our load, side by side."

With one arm around each other we throw our other arms high in the air as our routine comes to an end. We give each other a great big hug as the audience gives us a standing ovation.

The camera goes back to Joela Fountaine. "That was amazing! It looks like you guys still have it after all these years. I tell you, this has been an enlightening evening of conversation and entertainment. I like to thank Faith, Hope and Disparity for coming tonight and sharing their thoughts, memories and all those intriguing stories they have told us. Would you three like to stay and listen to what the rest of my guests have to say about St. Ann's Orphanage?" We, of course, were delighted to accept his invitation.

PATTY CAKE – BIG MISTAKE

"Our next guest comes to us from the middle 1950s. She, along with her siblings also spent part of their childhood years at St. Ann's Orphanage. Please give a warm welcome to Patty Cake."

Patty Cake made her way onto the stage and was greeted by Joela Fountaine. He escorted her to the couch next to his desk. Faith, Hope and Disparity had moved over to provide her with the seat next to Joela. They all hugged and finally settled in their comfortable seats.

"Thank you so much for joining us this evening Patty."

"Believe me, I am so excited to be here. When I found out my good friends, Faith, Hope and Disparity, were going to be on your show, I couldn't resist being part of this special occasion."

"We would like to hear a story or two about some of the events that happened at St. Ann's Orphanage during your stay. I see you can hardly wait to tell us some good stuff."

"Yes, Joela. It's story time and I'd like to start off with the infamous doo at the pool."

Faith burst out laughing. "Oh my god. That's a good one to start off with Patty. Who could forget that day?"

A picture of the pool is posted on the monitor for the audience to see. "You're right Faith. It was a beautiful, warm summer day in 1950 something. A large group of boys and girls were enjoying the afternoon splashing about the pool. Around the pool nuns were perched in their lawn chairs looking after the youngsters. Other kids were taking turns riding the few of the bicycles that were available. Some just mulled about the area while smaller groups took a leisurely stroll around the circular walkway."

"Pardon the expression, but all of a sudden it seemed like all hell broke loose. Kids in the pool were screaming and frantically trying to get out of the pool. There was this floating

140

object moving about the pool. Someone had done a no-no in the pool. We look back on the incident and laugh. But then, it was, well, hysterical! When everyone realized what it was you couldn't help but roll in laughter."

"That was until the sisters started in. Little did we know that something so... Well, let's just say, innocent would end up making so many kids unhappy."

"The kids that were in the pool were lined up along the walkway. Those not in the pool were quickly marched back to the dormitory building where they remained in the large playrooms. A nun slowly walked up and down the line of bathers banging her stick against her palm. She sternly looked each one in the eye asking if he or she was the devil who did this unspeakable deed."

"All the children were strong. No one admitted to the indiscretion which only made the sisters angrier. All the children that were in the pool that afternoon were banned for quite a while from enjoying anything to do with the pool area. That meant, no swimming, hanging out, walking, biking, skating or sitting about the pool area."

"You know, Joela. I wouldn't doubt it if someday this little incident is used in a movie. Just wait and see."

"You are so right Patty. Hollywood would just love to have something like this in one of their comedy movies. I guess we'll just have to wait and see. Are there any more stories for us?"

"Of course there are. None as intriguing as that story, though."

IT'S SUMMER TIME

"Summer time was a wonderful time. The warm weather gave us more opportunities to be outside. I've already mentioned the super pool we had. But we were offered many interesting, fun filled things to do. Staying in the confines of the 150-acre orphanage grounds still provided us with a plethora of adventures."

"Taking nature walks in small groups gave us time to solidify lifelong friendships. The topic of conversation would depend on the age of the group. Without us realizing it, we were taking in all the beauty of the world. Besides the incredible views that were offered us from our hillside retreat we were introduced to all that mother nature had to offer. The trees, wild flowers growing in the fields, plants blooming in the gardens and the different animals that were maintained at the orphanage."

"The older kids were able to roam a bit further from the orphanage. They had to be of good standing and in a group. Near the end of Granite Street was a corner store that sold penny candy. If a relative gave you some money, you were able to go to the store and buy some of those goodies. More than likely you would share with the few friends that were with you. Mind you, spend what you want, but eat what you buy before returning to the farm. If you didn't, what you had remaining would be confiscated and gone forever."

"Sometimes we would just hang about the back porches where we would sit at some table and play board games or go to an open floor area and play jacks. Some of us did like to sit back and read a good story. Of course, when it was raining the porches and play rooms would be full of kids. We all made the best of our situations."

"On the occasional lazy, hazy, crazy days of summer we would go on picnics. Sometimes just across the street behind the grotto. Other times larger groups of us would go on a bus to one of the many beautiful parks in Worcester. The older girls were allowed to go to dances and night shows in Worcester. There were no older boys to accompany them since no boys over age twelve were allowed to stay at St. Ann's."

"We all liked the new playgrounds that had been rebuilt for us. It was dedicated on September 16, 1951. The playground in the back of the dormitory building was for the little girls and the one next to it was for the younger boys. Two larger playgrounds were at the side of the buildings heading towards the pool area. There was a ballfield in one and a tennis and volley ball court in the other."

"As with any child playing outside, someone was bound to fall down and hurt themselves. Between the two lower playgrounds was a short driveway that had a slight slope to it. I believe more accidents happened there than most places in the playground. I

143

don't recall any broken bones, but there were plenty of scrapes and bruises and an occasional stitch or two."

THE SUMMER FESTIVAL

"The 1950s was the time for the summer festival held at Fitton field, Holy Cross College. Now this was something we all looked forward to. The festivals started in 1951 and lasted the decade. If you were lucky enough, you not only got to go to the festival but be an integral part of it by performing for the thousands of people who were there. That's right, I said thousands of people."

"Take 1959 for example. On June 22 the eighth Annual Stadium Festival was held at Fitton field, Holy Cross College. A group of ten younger kids performed a 'Let's Go Dutch' dance. They all looked so cute in their Dutch costumes. They even wore the classic wooden clogs. Later, an older group of children presented a hula-hoop routine. Both groups were directed by the long time dancing instructor, Miss Doris Joyce."

"The best part of the festival was the opportunity to personally meet the featured performers. Just think how excited the kids were to get their picture taken with Dick Clark of TV's 'American Bandstand'. The girls were ecstatic about being so close to teen idol Fabian. During the show they had prize drawings. A boy and girl from the orphanage was chosen to help Dick and Fabian pick the prize winners."

"What about the other years? Well, how about meeting Annette Funicello from the Mickey Mouse Club? Her birthday was on October 22, the same day as Faith's. There was the group of young dancers dressed all in white with white shoes and red soles. One of the little boys got stage fright when he saw the huge crowd, stopped dancing and started to cry. Annette ran onto the stage and rescued him. Her mere presence calmed him down and he was able to finish the performance."

"Connie Francis was one of the crowd's favorite female singers. She had a Catholic upbringing and sang many beautiful Christian songs. She, of course, sang 'Who's Sorry Now', her first big hit. Perry Como made quite a stir when he appeared on stage. I know many kids, including Faith and Hope, met and had their pictures taken with him. I think you wouldn't be surprised if I told you the nuns' favorite song was 'Ave Maria' beautifully sung by both Connie Francis and Perry Como."

TAKE ME OUT TO THE BALLGAME

Joela made a comment about the next piece about to be shown on the monitors. "I see we are about to put some home movies up on our monitors. I believe it's about a trip to Fenway Park. Hope, can you give us a narrative as we watch these?"

"I'll be delighted to. These home movie clips were collected from some of the folks who helped escort a group of children from the Worcester area, including St. Ann's Orphanage. Some parts have sound so I won't interrupt those segments."

"As you can see on the monitors there is a large crowd of kids getting ready to board a large number of buses. Boy, those kids really look excited. Oh, right there is a group of kids from St. Ann's Orphanage. There's Father Alfred and some of the nuns with him. Look how well behaved the kids are. Nicely lined up with a partner while the other groups' kids are just mulling about."

"We've jumped to the interior of the bus. I hear sounds, so let's listen in. It looks like one of the sisters is speaking. 'OK children, now that we're on our way I think we should practice our seventh inning stretch song. Ready, one, two, three. Take me out to the ballgame....'

The sound fades away as we watch a later clip. "Here they are disembarking from the bus. It looks like they're heading for the left grandstands gate. I'm guessing this is the first time that most of these kids have been to Fenway Park or even Boston. Look at those faces, priceless."

"There's the Green Monster. Did you know that the Green Monster was originally built of wood and in 1934 they covered it with metal plates and added the manual scoreboard that we still see today? Look over there in right field. See that red seat in the middle of the right field bleachers? That's where Ted Williams hit a home run that was over five hundred feet from home plate."

"This next clip shows them gathering on the field. That's right, this was the time these kids were invited to meet with some of the players because of all the help they did for the Jimmy Fund. Let me explain while we watch. In 1948 a twelve-year old boy was receiving treatment from the Dana Farber Cancer Institute in Boston. While in the hospital he asked for a TV so he could watch his favorite team, the Boston Braves. Word got out and before long over $200,000 was raised. Thus, started the Jimmy Fund."

"Oh, look there, I believe that's Ted Williams. I see number nine taking pictures with some of the kids and signing baseballs for them. Look out there in right field. See the bullpen. They call that Williamsburg since Ted has hit so many home runs into it. I don't see it here, but I heard the kids sang the Star Spangled Banner right after they met the players."

"The next part is a slideshow of the kids back up in the grand stands. I see they are all settling in with all kinds of goodies. How could you go to a ballgame and not get a tonic (soda to others), a bag of peanuts, a hot dog or two and a box of Cracker

Jacks? Look, in the background you can see the game is underway. There's Ted Williams way out there in left field. Boy, I wish I was there."

"It looks like we have more video. Let's listen in. 'Ladies and gentlemen, let's all stand for the seventh inning stretch and sing our favorite baseball song, Take me out to the ballgame.' You can see these kids are really enjoying themselves. They sound really good after all their practice."

"Now we see them back on their busses heading back to Worcester. Look, half of them are chatting away with big smiles on their faces and the others are sleeping. It looks like they all had a wonderful day at the park."

The monitors go dark and the audience gives a big applause.

TIDBITS OF MEMORIES

Joela Fountaine. "Boy, that was a great presentation. I can almost taste the ball park franks. Well, I'm sure there are other tidbits of stories still worth mentioning. Faith, could you help us with some you may remember?"

"Sure Joela. There was this one particular nun who watched over us at night and loved to play 'Open Up Your Heart and Let the Sunshine In.' on her record player. As soon as she went into her room at the end of the dormitory we would hear it playing. This song tells you the devil causes trouble when you let him in the room. So remember, 'Smilers never lose and frowners never win. So let the sun shine in, face it with a grin.'

148

"We would fall asleep listening to that awful song and dream of the devil trying to get into the window with all the fire and brimstone he could muster. He would come and take us away if we didn't smile and think happy thoughts. We had nightmares because of it. Whenever we heard this song fear would permeate through our little bodies."

Patty said. "What about those holy pictures and statues they had strategically placed around the buildings. There was this one of Jesus. His eyes seemed to follow you wherever you went. Boy, did that ever scare the living crap out of me! No matter how hard I tried to ignore him I couldn't help but watch his eyes follow me. Sometimes, I would run past him to see if I could get past without his eyes meeting mine. It never happened."

Faith had a flash back moment. "Jeepers, I just remember something from our classroom days. You see, I do everything left handed. I believe you're a lefty too. Right Patty?"

"Yeah, I think I know where you're going with this Faith."

"You see, the nuns did not like anyone who was left handed. They actually tied our hands behind our backs, making us use only our right hands. According to some kind of myth or something, lefties have the devil in them. It is said that left handed people have been linked to many bad things, such as: the mark of the devil, a sign of neurosis, nasty habits, rebellion, criminality and homosexuality, just to name a few. The word 'left' actually comes from the Anglo-Saxon word 'lyft', which means weak or broken. So, of course, the nuns believed all this garbage. It did them no good. I am still a lefty, so beware!"

Every one laughs off the severity of Faith's statement as she changes the subject. "You know summer time wasn't the only fun time of the year. We did manage to find a diverse amount of things to help entertain us in the off season. We actually got to go to the movies. You already heard about skating on the pool. Sledding down those hills around the farm was always a great way to enjoy the outdoors after a snow storm. We used to make some pretty good looking snowmen too."

Patty said. "Oh yah. Wintertime did bring about the flu and lots of kids got colds. With nearly two hundred of us, how could you not get a cold? Colds were remedied the old fashion way, with Vicks Vapor rub. The nuns used to put a gauze pad full of the stuff on your chest. Then they would slap it in and around your nostrils. A Vicks cough drop would then be administered. Kids would swear that the nuns dipped them in that vapor rub before making them eat it."

Faith said. "Since we went to school in the orphanage you would think that we wouldn't get lice. But one year it spread around the little girls' dormitory. The nuns figured it was brought in by one of the new girls. A nun would take one of those awful metal lice combs and scan each one of the girl's scalps. If you were found to have just one nit or louse, you would go through a vigorous head scrubbing. This stuff used to burn our scalps when they scrubbed it in. Once done, you had to go through another scalp scan to insure all the lice were eradicated. That was not a fun time. Especially if you did have lice. The kids would point at you yelling, she's got COOTIES!"

Patty came back with another tidbit. "If you had straight hair, you would get the straight box cut. Simple enough to do. Get a pair of scissors and make a straight cut just above your eyebrows for the bangs. Then make another straight cut for the hair line somewhere between the shoulders and the ears. Done! Ah, what I would have given to have naturally curly hair. Maybe those new rock-n-roll bands will start wearing their hair like ours. Yeah, yeah, yeah."

BIRTHDAY CAKE FOR EVERYBODY

Hope inserted another bit of information. "I had the chicken pox when I was there. I remember getting special treatment. They would dab that calamine lotion all over me a couple times a day. There was no scratching. If I did as I was told, I was given ice cream. It was actually a fun time for me even if I did have to stay in bed all day for a few days. I guess it must have been the attention I was getting. It had been a long time since I got that."

Patty concluded. "You know, many of the kids were curious and would talk about the sisters. I remember asking one if they ate food. I used to ask them questions about their hair, if they had any, etc. One time a nun let me touch her white collar and habit. It didn't feel soft at all. They also let us touch their prayer beads that hung down their skirts. Some of the girls even wanted to be nuns so they could wear the habits because they thought they were really neat. We were all curious about what could be in their rooms that we were prohibited from entering."

"We heard that the older girls who had been at the orphanage forever were given special chores. Depending on how good they were depended on what special chore they were assigned to. Taking responsibility for the nuns' aprons, learning and working side by side with the cook in the kitchen. Taking care of Father Alfred's room or assisting the nuns with theirs were a few privileges they got."

CHRISTMAS EXTRAVAGANZA

Joela Fountaine made the next introduction. "Thank you all for your inputs. I bet we could go on all evening. But it's time to meet our next guest. During the Christmas season the orphanage would pose quite a dilemma. With nearly two hundred children to provide gifts for, you can imagine only one sanctioned being could pull it off. So tonight we bring you the man himself, straight from the Worcester Gazette. The man who put a lot of smiles on the children of St. Ann's Orphanage. Ladies and gentlemen, Santa Claus."

Santa entered the stage calling out, "Ho, ho, ho. Hello to all my dear little friends in TV land." After greeting the other guests, he sat down. "What a great looking crowd I see tonight. I am so happy to tell you a story or two of my stop overs at St. Ann's Orphanage. They are such a wonderful group of children. When I entered that large auditorium with so many children, I could feel the instant change come over them as those sad little faces turned to joy."

Joela asked. "Santa, is there one particular Christmas visit to St. Ann's you really enjoyed?"

"Well, let me think. Why don't I tell you about 1954? That was a real special year. About 150 children from St. Ann's Orphanage came to Santa Land at the Lincoln Plaza in downtown Worcester. They all had their picture taken with Santa as he talked to each one of them. They gave him three choices for a gift they would like to receive. That way Santa was able to get a good idea of what they really wanted for Christmas."

"As we adults know Santa could not do this all on his own. Assistance came from many businesses, charities and benefactors along with individuals from Worcester and the surrounding communities. They helped provide the many hundreds of gifts needed to make this and all the other Christmases a happy and special one."

"Just a few days before Christmas Eve the children at St. Ann's Orphanage welcomed the Worcester Gazette Santa, that was me (Willard S. Smith), to their annual Christmas party. The program opened with a lovely cantata pageant 'Bernadette of Lourdes'. It was beautifully and reverently sung and acted by the senior girls under the musical direction of Raymond A. Galipeau.

The wee folks entertained the audience with a delightful snowman dance directed by Miss Doris Joyce. I do remember that your guests, Faith and Hope, were in that song and dance number."

"Anyway, the program concluded with, of course, the arrival of Santa. I came onto the stage and showed those kids a few bits of magic. I think the adults enjoyed it as much as the kids. Finally, it was time for distributing the gifts and candy. I sat on stage in a big chair and called out each child's name and presented them with at least one of the gifts they had asked for. Those were very precious moments."

"I believe Bishop Wright, Msgr. David C. Sullivan and Rev. Alfred Berthiaume were present to say a few prayers and share in the Christmas gallantry. Many family members and local residents also came to this festive occasion. When the gifts were all opened and the party came to a close I said my goodbyes and headed back to the North Pole. I understand that most of the children were fortunate enough to go home to spend the remainder of the holidays with their families or selective hosts."

"That Christmas was just as wonderful and delightful as all the other years I visited St. Ann's. There is nothing so fulfilling as to see a happy child. These children all had something to be sad about and at least for this special season we tried to ease the pain."

"I'm sorry Mr. Fountaine, but I must head back to the North Pole. There are more and more children being added to my list for this upcoming Christmas. Thank you for inviting me today. Ho, ho, ho, I must go. Remember everyone, be good and kind and your wishes will be fulfilled."

Joela Fountaine smiled and said. "Laying his finger aside of his nose, he gave a nod and up the chimney he rose. Oh, sorry, wrong story. Good night Santa."

Joela Fountaine turned to his remaining guests and asked. "It has been mentioned by some folks that after the Christmas holidays the gifts were taken away from the children. Is this a true statement?"

Hope tried to answer the question. "Well, that is both true and a bit misleading. You see, some of the gifts were indeed taken away. Things like a sled or a bicycle, maybe even a basketball may have been confiscated. It was deemed necessary for these type of gifts to become community property. Since not every child could individually have one of these gifts they had to be shared."

"I know it might seem unfair, but that way all the children had the opportunity to ride a bike, or take a sled ride down the hill. Board games, jacks, jump ropes and such also became part of the community property. On the other hand, the smaller, personalized gifts would have been allowed to be kept by a child. Little girl's dolls were an example, as long as every girl had their own."

"Some of the children who went home for the holidays felt it necessary to leave their new toys at home. That way they would not have their gifts appropriated and put into the community toy basket. I guess that's the best explanation we can give."

Joela responded. "I see. I guess the lesson there is, 'if you got it hide it. Next up, a special tribute."

ST. ANN'S AND FATHER ALFRED 1938-1970

Joela begins the tribute. "St. Ann's Orphanage is blessed with a very special person, in the name of Farther Alfred (Roland) Berthiaume. He has been an integral part of the orphanage since he replaced Father Yvon L' Floc'h in 1938. Let's watch the monitors as we pay tribute to this amazing man."

Since 1938 Father Alfred Berthiaume has been the chaplain of St. Ann's Orphanage and Mount St. Ann. He went to the orphanage on almost a daily basis. He heard confessions, presided over masses and celebrated the Eucharist. He retired in 1970 but for the next 10 years, before falling ill and passing away in 1981, he continued to be an integral part of Mount St. Ann.

156

Many people who were very young have few memories of the time they spent at St. Ann's but Father Alfred's name is one of those memories. Many boys remember being altar boys for him. Girls would become flower girls for him and Bishop Wright.

Father Alfred would be there year after year to perform every child's first communion. One child recalled, "I had the mumps and couldn't attend First Holy Communion. Father Alfred brought me an unblessed host so I could practice making my first communion. When I was better he performed a private ceremony for me. This was one of the best days of my life." He also assisted Bishop Wright performing confirmations to those who were of age.

This was one priest who took extra time to be with his young flock. He was a kind and gentle man who actually enjoyed their company. It didn't matter if you were not a Catholic or of some another race. You were part of his flock and he cared for each and every one of you.

He welcomed you into his home and introduced you to his family. Many girls made lifelong friends with his niece, Paulette Berthiaume. She once stated. "My uncle was Father Alfred Berthiaume. When I was a young girl he would bring a group of children from the orphanage to an annual picnic at our house in Spenser, Ma. We always looked forward to those picnics."

One girl made this statement in a note to Paulette that rings true for many of us. "I just wanted to let you know how much I loved and appreciated your uncle, Father Alfred. I have very fond memories of him. He used to bring us to your house where I met you. You and your family were so nice to all us girls. He used to drive us around playing Rock and Roll music on the radio. He took us swimming, to get ice cream and to your house, sometimes other friends' houses. He used to give us rides to the dances and then pick us up."

"He was the greatest, I would never have enjoyed my stay there as much as I did if it weren't for your uncle. I was given the responsibility of taking your uncle's breakfast, lunch and dinner to him. Every weekend I was tasked to change the linens in his room. These where the best chores of all the chores they had for us girls. I was honored to do these things for him and really happy and felt lucky that I was chosen. I just wanted to let you know how much he was appreciated and well liked. I'm sure many other children felt the same."

Father Alfred escorted kids to football games at Holy Cross and some kids even met with Bob Cousy of the Celtics at Boston Garden. Let's not forget the Red Sox games. He took others to Assumption College to see the Nut Cracker Ballet and other performances.

To others he was the man with the answers. Definitely the father figure no one really had. He would literally let the kids 'Knock on wood' since he indeed had a wooden leg.

All in all, Father Alfred was a man of the cloth. He knew how much these children were hurting and tried to ease their pain as well as he could. Listen to this child tell her story of pain and comfort.

"After masses on Sunday Father Alfred took me to see my mother, who was sick with cancer. One Sunday as we left she died. On the way back to the cottages he took me to the chapel. I remember his words of comfort. He told me my mother had taken her place in heaven. He and Sister Helen helped me deal with my mother's passing."

"Father Alfred was a godsend to me at one of my darkest hours. Had it not been for him, his counsel and care, I know I would have lost total faith in God. To this day I carry with me what he told me the day my mother passed. 'Your mother is out of pain and in God's loving arms. She promised she will watch over you from heaven and that when you see a rainbow it will be her smiling down on you. God will protect and guide you. Keep your faith in Him. Promise me you will pray daily and heaven will help you find peace.' I promised him I would. He gave me a big hug and let me cry. We just sat there in the church for what seemed like hours. I wrote down the conversation in my journal and took it with me when I left."

Father Alfred is a true man of God - An angel in disguise! Say a prayer for him tonight. Amen

Joela Fountaine. "Very nice. It almost seemed like the tribute was a bit futuristic. Anyway, I have no doubt Father Alfred will be with this organization for many more years to come."

SISTER GRAY & FATHER BROWN

Joela Fountaine. "Speaking of Priests, Let's bring on Father Brown and Sister Gray. Since so much has been said about the sisters and the clergy I felt it was only fitting that they have a say in the matters of St. Ann's Orphanage. So, without further ado, Sister Gray and Father Brown."

Sister Gray and Father Brown enter the stage and are greeted by Joela and all the guests. Once the applause has quieted and everyone has settled Joela asks. "Sister Gray, it has been said that the nuns were insensitive and distant with the children in their charge. Can you give us your insight to these remarks?"

"First of all, let me thank you for inviting us to be part of you show. Many people believe us to be monsters, mean spirited, or just plain indignant toward the children we serve. This is far from true. As they say, there are two sides to every story. Our side seems to be a bit tarnished so Father Brown and I would like to give it a good shine."

"Our facility would constantly be housing about 200 children. It was like a revolving door. On average you would see one child enter and one child depart every other day. It was quite different than a school where a group of children would come in at the beginning of a semester and remain for the year. Their names would be known within a few days. Throughout the year you would get to know much more about each individual. At St. Ann's this was at best difficult and in most cases didn't happen."

"Many of the children came and went so quickly we could not memorize each and every one of them. Those who remained in our care for a lengthy stay would create a special bond with one or more of the sisters. It did not mean the sisters did not care, or love, the short timers. These nuns' lives are dedicated to caring for all the children. It is in their nature and their vows. The sisters were not insensitive toward them. As I said, it just takes time to truly bond with someone."

"Children take different amounts of time to adjust to their new home. Many things account for this. The most profound issue with adjustment had to do with the children who were the closest to one, or both of their parents. They were the ones who would show signs of deep sadness and despair. But eventually most of them would find their new home tolerable, if only for the moment."

"Every so often we would get a child that just wasn't responsive to his or her new surroundings. These children were beyond reproach. We found it best to quickly get these children into an adoptive home. That way their adjustment would be less traumatic. So you see, we do care for all the children's wellbeing."

"The 1950s brought many challenges to our orphanage. Times had changed and we needed to change too. It was slow going at first. Our first challenge came in the early months of 1951. The provincial administration headquarters of the Grey Nuns (The Sisters of Charity) for the United States was moved to St. Ann's. This meant high ranking sisters, clergymen and administrative personnel were presiding at the site in close proximity to the day to day lives of the children."

"This intrusion may have created a sense of urgency. The children were constantly reminded to be on their best behavior. More performances were required and more publicity came our way. It was a large order to handle. The children performed on radio and TV. They went to different organizations around the Worcester area to perform. The summer festival was the grandest of them all."

"This did not mean an increase in discipline. By all means there were rules for punishment. Over the past seventy years carrying out specific punishments has been adjusted to comply with all surrounding institutions, including public schools. If you were to go into nearby homes that have a husband and wife component, you would see some of the same punishments, some more severe. Our punishments may be looked upon as unjustifiable only because of the sheer number of children involved."

"Like any family, we admit that some members were more inclined to raise a hand or punish first then ask questions later. Some children would go as far as to say this nun or that was very mean. Yet, other nuns were very nice. Whether at home, in school or in this orphanage it is about instilling discipline within the child. It is, and always will be, a necessary evil."

"Very interesting view on a touchy subject. Well spoken, Sister Gray." said Joela. "Can you tell us about the other responsibilities of the nuns, novices and employees of St. Ann's Orphanage?"

"Of course. As many know, we are incorporated in the State of Massachusetts as the St. Ann's French Canadian Orphanage. As a business we have many responsibilities. First and foremost, is the care we have sworn to uphold. The first page of our Minutes of Incorporation dated February 27, 1892 simply states the reason for its establishment: '…for the maintenance, care and education of orphan children, for the care and support of aged invalids, for giving and comfort, shelter and medical treatment to the sick and suffering, and for visiting the sick and helping the needy.' It was signed by the seven founding sisters of St. Ann's French Canadian Orphanage."

"This business was more complicated than most. This was much more than a home for lost souls living on a working farm. Like many large companies we had different divisions. There were animals to be raised, fed, slaughtered and prepared for eating today and tomorrow. Our produce department prepared the fields, sowed the seed, and harvested the crops. They also managed whatever fruits we had growing on the farm."

"Our processing division consisted of employed women, hired hands and the children who were capable of assisting in the preservation of these crops. Maintaining the fields was a chore done by the boys with the guidance of hired field hands. Gathering fire wood for the winter was also a big task since our furnaces and fireplaces had an enormous appetite during the cold winter months."

"Another division dealt with the solicitation of funds that would provide us cash or other needed items we could not reap from our fields. This was not an easy task. It was very important to enlist as many benefactors as we could. Their help was detrimental to our survival."

"You could say we were also a hotel management group. The responsibilities here are boundless. Preparing the sleeping quarters, laundry and ironing facilities, food preparation and dining for over two hundred guests. Landscaping and overall outward and inward appearances."

"We required a marketing division to help buy and sell goods. Things like cloth and sewing materials were absolutely necessary to keep our charges properly fitted. Selling items that we made and grew was an important way to increase our coffers. Our financial division had to keep a strict account of all our assets, income and sales of our goods."

"I apologize if I left out any important areas. But you can see there are many divisions within the corporation of St. Ann's Orphanage. To think that approximately fifteen nuns handled all these divisions is amazing in itself. The Grey Nuns were, and still are the management team. I have nothing but high praise for their efforts in maintaining this institution over these many decades."

The audience and guests applauded Sister Gray's remarks. Joela Fountaine looked toward Father Brown. "Father Brown, you seem anxious to tell us something. Would you like to speak?

"Yes. I would like to start off with a direct response to possible sexual abuse that may have occurred in St. Ann's Orphanage. I can tell you in good faith that we know nothing of this and that no one has come forward. There have never been any reports to these or any similar allegations. Long after children have left the orphanage they see things they believe may have happened to them in their past. It is only normal that their memories can get convoluted."

"It has been mentioned on numerous occasions that our charges come to us from many different home lives. We always hear about the tragic tales of losing a loved one. The abusive stories are shunned and not discussed. These children also come from or are returned to family or adoptive homes where the child has been abused, mentally, physically or sexually. The children grow up with this stigma and push it deep into their subconscious only to later have a partial memory rekindled by some new event. They may comingle previous incidents with the idea that our orphanage may have had a part in it."

"Until just recently, we didn't realize the ramifications of these hidden emotions. A good example of this is when the clergy would go to St. Ann's to see a stage show or be part of a special event. We would have the young performers come sit on our laps. We would hug and praise them for the good job they did on stage. We didn't realize their distain they had toward this approach until years had passed. Some told us how uncomfortable they had felt. A male figure was one of their suppressed emotions they could not accept."

"We now have a better understanding of these situations and the sixties promise to being a new format in child care. There will be psychologists, therapists and councilors to help these children cope with any traumatic situations they may have.

Separation anxieties from their families and siblings, along with any physical or psychological conditions will now be addressed."

"With that said, I would like to go over the transition St. Ann's Orphanage has experienced during the 1950s. The start of the 1950s showed the resident population at St. Anne's Orphanage to be about 185 to 200 with boys ages 4-12 and girls ages 4-16. Schooling was still provided up to the sixth grade. Then they attended either St. Joseph's Parochial School or Ascension High School."

"The type of children began to change. The true 'orphan' turned to single parent boarders, unwanted and rejected children. The farm could no longer maintain itself with pigs and chickens. To keep up with the costs, St. Ann's gladly took in these boarders for a fee. The sisters felt their care would be preferable to the child's home situation."

"As a more diverse population emerged around Worcester so did the children entering St. Ann's Orphanage. It became apparent that French was no longer the language of choice and English was the language of necessity. Even the new nuns that came to St. Ann's had English as their primary language."

"By 1957 many discussions were held about institutions like St. Ann's Orphanage. Denigrating descriptions were being tossed around. "The institution is a monster." To "The institution is a panacea, or remedy." To the middle-ground, "It is useful in certain circumstances." A survey of agencies in Worcester recommended that the administration had to quickly move to transform St. Ann's into an institution in which both charity and sound concepts of child care are present."

"1959 became the decisive year when the Director of Catholic Charities, the Reverend Timothy J. Harrington, directed a change in the emphasis of the orphanage. New Concepts and approaches in child care would be implemented. This meant changing from a non-selective policy to a selective policy. St. Ann's would no longer be paid as a babysitting service for the public."

"As a result, a full screening of each child's needs would take place. The number of children residing at St. Ann's will be drastically reduced. This is a milestone that will re-focus the total program of St. Ann's Orphanage. The sisters will now be educated in the institutional child-care approach."

"As a final note I would like to tell you that the next ten years will bring a profound change to St. Ann's French Canadian Orphanage. Orphanages are quickly becoming passé and the new progression is toward the foster care system. I suggest you all keep a close watch on the events that will unfold throughout the 1960s."

IT'S TIME TO SAY GOOD NIGHT

Joela Fountaine. "I hate to say it but our time in the 1950s is just about up. The clock ticks closer to the end of this decade and soon rings in the new. It was a decade that brought about major world events, like the Soviet sputnik entering space. The cold war is now brewing and fears of a nuclear holocaust looms upon our doorsteps."

"Television entered our homes, bringing the vision radio could not supply us. The economy of our nation has given the normal man the affordability to buy a new car and a home for his growing family. With the advent of the National Highway System, introduced by President Dwight D. Eisenhower, we can now visit family and friends across the country."

"As we watch the last few seconds of the 1950s tick away we can only hope the decade of the 60s continues to bring us peace and prosperity. I would like to thank my guests, Faith, Hope, Disparity, Patty Cake, Father Christmas, Sister Gray and Father Brown. The music group Depth of Despair, my announcer and lifelong friend Rosie Rivet, the Orphan Show Band, and especially all the people who make this program so special. Good-night and Happy New Year."

We all call out, 'Happy New Year' as well. The audience applauds as the Orphan Band plays the theme song. Midnight strikes calling in 1960 as the fireworks snap, crackle, and pop on all the monitors. Joela shakes hands with all his guests, waves to the crowd, then departs the stage. The guests in turn also depart the stage to their dressing rooms.

As we settled into some chairs set up in our dressing room the television turned itself on again. We hear that male, monotone voice emanating from the speakers.

'The characters we have encountered have allowed us to hear the minds and souls of those less fortunate. Opening their hearts and souls to the multitude can bring ambivalent results. The essence of humility lacking in their counterparts has caused these young souls to travel life's journey into the depths of despair and disquiet. We now return control of your television set to you, until next time when we take you to… The Outer Limits of the Twilight Zone.'

168

"Wow," said Rosalie. "now that was a TV show! I think we learned a lot about the kids and people involved at St. Ann's. I can't wait to see how we get through the 1960s."

Chapter 9

The Eve of Destruction

ALICES RESTAURANT

We helped ourselves to tea and brownies laid out for us on a nearby table. I said. "I guess we can enjoy a little nosh and repose while we wait for our next encounter of the weird kind. Don't you guys think this journey to the center of our minds has been incredible so far?"

Rosalie was enjoying her second brownie but was able to mumble. "Mmmmm, incredible is right. So are these brownies!" Christine only managed a nod or two as she too had a mouthful of brownie. We continued to indulge in these great tasting morsels until we had satisfied our new found hunger.

As we lay back in our seats the room lights created a ménage of colors swirling about. Psychedelic music invaded our ears and enveloped our minds. For a few moments we did not move while we took in a new motility. This feeling of awareness took a strong hold on us. I believe we are about to enter the center of our minds.

The door opened and a vision came to us. "Hello my friends. My name is Alice and this is Sky, your pilot. We have come to help navigate you along the final paths of St. Ann's Orphanage. Your trip will bring you to the eve of destruction and the dawn of a new age. While one diminishes the physicality and philosophies of the past, the other will inspire a rebirth that will preserve the oath made so long ago in 1892."

"Hi, as your Sky Pilot, I ask you, how high can you fly and never reach the sky? Let yourselves be taken by the intertwining hues of your minds while you listen to the sounds of silence. Encircle your thoughts and open your minds, for we can fly up, up and away to the reality of St. Ann's Orphanage during the 1960s. It's time to get a ticket to ride upon your magic swirling ship."

"Each of you will be transported in the vessel your subconscious has chosen. Rosalie, while you relax in your easy chair I will control the path of your home as it twists about the clouds heading for that place over the rainbow. Christine will journey in her blue police box as I maneuver it through time and relative dimension in space. Joseph will sit upon the bridge of his starship and boldly go where he may not have gone before."

We continued to relax in our seats, not saying a word as visons began filling our subconscious minds. Each of us saw what Sky introduced to our minds. We met our new found experience with enthusiasm. We focused in on our individual encounters in anticipation of meeting the early days of the 1960s.

UP, UP AND AWAY

Rosalie envisions herself sitting in front of a large window. She feels the sensation of a monstrous tornado engulfing her home, lifting her high into the atmosphere. She grabs hold of her little dog Mollie just as the windows explode outward revealing the inside of the twister.

"Jeepers, Mollie, I guess Dorothy was right. We aren't in Kansas anymore or Worcester for that fact. Oh, look. Did you see that? I think I just saw Christine fly by inside a blue phone booth. No, it says 'Police Box' on the outside. I think they call that thing a Tardis. Wow, look over there. There goes a starship. I bet Joe is on board that thing. This trip is going to be amazing!"

Christine finds herself inside the infinite confines of the TARDIS - Time and Relative Dimension in Space. In the center of the ship is the control station with Sky as the pilot. Some may refer to him as 'The Doctor'. The TARDIS possesses telepathic circuits that can accommodate whomever needs assistance while being transported through space and time. She is in an anteroom relaxing in her comfortable chair.

"I feel like I'm about to witness some brilliant stories from the 1960s. Oh my, the Tardis is connecting me to a neural network of the children's' minds. Now that's what they called 'heavy' back in the 60s. I see, I can tune into whichever child I choose. I can't wait to visit with as many of them as I can."

I find myself on board a starship. There is a special chair beside the captain's just for me. We are sitting in the middle of a circular bridge with console stations behind us. In front is a half-moon shaped desk with two officers manning the numerous controls. I turned and looked behind me to see if there happened to be a man with pointed ears.

THE DAWN OF A GOLDEN AGE

Sky, was sitting in the captain's chair and directed me to an enormous monitor in front of us. "Mr. Joe, from here we can bear witness to the events of the St. Ann's Orphanage during the 1960s. This decade will be the decade of destruction and rebirth of the ideals that transcended the lifespan of St. Ann's French Canadian Orphanage."

The large viewer turned on to reveal a large table with about ten to fifteen adults and a couple nuns sitting around it. We hear them discussing the situations at St. Ann's and what is needed to correct them. A slide show is presented to the board. We are witnessing the implementation of new concepts and approaches in child care. As promised, the sisters are re-evaluating each of the children in their care. The decrease in the surplus population at St. Ann's Orphanage has begun. The sisters are sent to be educated in the institutional child-care approach.

My comment was brief. "I remember the beginning of the 60s was a sign of great things to come. But we all know that was not to be."

Rosalie is intrigued by the spectacle before her. Music history of the early 60s is unfolding within the massive wind storm in front of her. A collage of music begins to entertain her. "Look Mollie, there's Chubby Checker singing and dancing to 'The Twist'. That was number one in 1960 and again in 1962. I believe he started the dance craze of the 60s. There was 'Pony Time', 'The Hucklebuck' and 'Limbo Rock'."

"Look there, that's American Bandstand. That was really popular. Dick Clark really knew how to get the young teen generation dancing. He even came to the summer festivals in

Worcester. See, the kids are up and dancing the 'Mash Potato' while Dee Dee Sharp sings. We still hear the 'Monster Mash' every Halloween on the radio. You know Elvis had just come back from his tour of duty and had a couple hits, too. 'Are You Lonesome Tonight' was one of his songs." Elvis went flying by singing 'It's Now or Never.'

Groups like the Shirelles, the Ronettes, the Marvelettes and the Chiffons flashed by her window singing snippets from their hit songs of the early 60s. Following the ladies' groups, Rosalie saw the Beach Boys, then Bobby Vinton singing 'Mr. Lonely' floating past her window.

The 1960s brought a new era of television programming. TV sets were getting more sophisticated. Black and white was now color. Comedy shows and lighthearted sitcoms became the shows to watch. The introductory scenes of many shows went flying by Rosalie's window. Dick Van Dyke falling over that strategically placed piece of furniture. Andy Griffith and Opie walking down the road with their fishing poles. There goes the burning map of the Ponderosa from the opening of Bonanza.

Next passes Lassie and the infamous heart from I Love Lucy. The moon from the Honeymooners zips across the horizon. My Three Sons, Leave it to Beaver, and Bewitched, on and on the shows pass by.

Some of the long running shows from the 1950s still had a large audience in the 60s. Passing by her window was The shootout at high noon from the opening of Gunsmoke and the calling card from Have Gun Will Travel. Finally, the stampede of cattle from Rawhide.

The scene changed from television episodes to historical events. The flag of the United States passes by showing off its new pattern of fifty stars. Rosalie watches as she sees four black college students from Greensboro, North Carolina stage a sit-in at a segregated Woolworth lunch counter in protest of their denial of service. It was 1960 and the civil rights movement was about to make historical strides.

The first presidential debate on television between John F. Kennedy and Richard W. Nixon makes an appearance. It is followed by John F. Kennedy speaking to the crowd at his inauguration. Rosalie hears a snippet of his address... 'Ask not what your country can do for you, ask what you can do for your country....'

Rocket ships are now blasting past her window as the race for outer space between the Soviet Union and the United States has begun. Kennedy floats by bellowing out his space program to 35,000 people at Rice Stadium. '...We choose to go to the Moon in this decade..., *not* because they are easy, *but because they are hard...*' Rosalie sees our astronauts head into space and turns to Mollie. "Wow, I remember seeing this on TV. Our elementary school had a television in the science room and they squeezed as many kids and teachers into the room as possible so we could witness those historical events."

The Berlin Wall floats upon the wind reminding all of us that there is a cold war going on between the U.S. and the Soviets. Again Rosalie comments. "We just saw a piece of the wall when we visited Montreal. We even got to stand right next to it and touch it. How cool is that?"

Now, United States troops are marching past heading to Viet Nam marking the beginning of an unwanted war. In turn, the Bay of Pigs presents itself followed by Kennedy's televised demand that the Soviet Union disband their missile sites secretly being installed on Cuban soil.

Martin Luther King, Jr. comes marching by with his peaceful protesting across the south. This is culminated by the Civil Rights march on Washington, DC. Demands for jobs and freedom are supported by over 200,000 people of all races walking arm in arm to the Lincoln Memorial. There they hear the famous 'I Have a Dream' speech.

A motorcade with John F. Kennedy and his wife Jacqueline pass through the streets of Dallas, Texas. This was a memory we all shared. I'm sure you can all remember where you were and what you were doing when you found out about this horrific deed.

IMPLIMENTING FOSTER CARE

Christine begins her journey selecting a sad girl around 6 years old who was leaving St. Ann's. Her thoughts reminisce about her short stay at the old orphanage. "I still see visions of how the older girls took care of us. They would take us to the spooky showers in the basement. We had to keep our panties on while showering. There was that big dining room we ate all our meals in."

"I still see the bath rooms lined up with sinks on one side and toilets on the other. We had to sleep in these white metal railing crib beds. I was there for one party at Christmas and got a big doll that looked like me. I cherished it and a stuffed elephant I had. But, like all the other kids I had to leave them behind when I left to go to a foster home."

Christine skips to another girl's thoughts. This one seems more upset than sad. It appears that with the implementation of foster care many of the children don't have a chance to bond with other children. Just when they do have a new confidant they are relocated without even a goodbye. Eventually, they are fed into the child care system.

The scene turns to the starship where Sky, the pilot gives the order to maneuver our starship over the island of Cuba. I gaze upon the screen to see missile sites strategically being built. Large groups of children are boarding airplanes while leaving their loving families behind. The St. Ann's board members start discussing another decisive matter.

"It has come to our attention that a group of Cuban refugees will be sent to St. Ann's. The parents have mounting fears that the Soviets and Castro will indoctrinate their children to strict communist ways. This is part of the Pedro Plan that hopes to bring about 14,000 children to the safety of the United States."

"The Cuban refugees will be sent ahead of their parents. We hope to eventually reunite them when, and if they get permission to come to the United States. Per our newly upgraded guidelines, plans are in the works to place these children in local foster homes without splitting up the siblings."

The starship pulls away from its position above Cuba and speeds to Worcester, Massachusetts as Christine's mind retakes hold of our journey.

Christine's next mind meld connects her with one of the ten Cuban refugees recently accepted to St. Ann's Orphanage. It is June 1962. Only two of the children speak some English but there are no issues with the telepathic interpretations. It is mail call for the children and one of the sisters is passing out letters to them. Christine listens to the thoughts of a sixteen-year-old girl.

"Today, we are getting letters from our family back in Havana, Cuba. It has been many months since we have seen them. We miss them so much. They tell us that Fidel Castro is not letting our families leave Cuba. We are told we may never see them again. We pray every day that this is not true."

"We are treated very well here. The priests and the sisters are good decent people who are caring for us during our trying times. We do not know what would have happened to us if St. Ann's Orphanage did not help. We will endeavor to be good children during our stay."

"It is time for me to read the letter from my madre and padre to my little sister. Come Hermanita where we can have a private moment while I read you our letter." Christine discontinued her connection to allow the two the privacy they seek.

THE BEGINNING OF THE END

The starship settled over the site of the orphanage. Sky reestablished a connection to the board room where the 1963 year-end meeting was taking place. If things were changing, it wasn't for the good of St. Ann's Orphanage.

"My dear colleagues, it has been a trying year for all of us. Just when we have trimmed the population of the institution and established ourselves as a formidable entity in the Massachusetts child care arena we end up with bad news after bad."

"As you all know earlier this year our facilities on Granite Street were found to be substandard. The main building was deemed unsafe and unhealthy. We were instructed to make plans to tear it down. Since the out buildings were no longer in use they were all immediately razed."

"Subsequently, the brick building had a fire in the furnace room. It appears that a steam pipe located above the boiler was too close to the ceiling and created the fire. It soon spread to a first floor room in the rear of the building destroying Christmas Gifts for the 37 children presently living there."

"Since the main building houses the kitchen and dining areas, the chapel and the administration operation of St. Ann's we have been given a reprieve. This does not mean we can continue without a plan for the future of St. Ann's Orphanage."

THE BRITISH ARE COMING

Rosalie is settling down in her spinning abode enjoying the historical sequences passing in front of her eyes. 'I Want to Hold Your Hand' invades her ears as the aperture in front of her is filled with the Fab Four Beatles. More British musical groups spin by as the Beatles remain in the background maintaining their stronghold on the music industry and youth of the 60s.

English groups like the Hollies, Jerry and the Pacemakers, Petula Clark, The Dave Clark Five and Herman's Hermits sing their hit songs as they swirl by. Duet groups like Chad and Jeremy and Peter and Gordon sing their memorable ballads. The House of the Rising Sun sung by the Animals and Satisfaction by the Rolling Stones make an appearance.

American groups that made dents in the British Invasion crossed the ruptured window. The Supremes, The Beach Boys, Sonny and Cher, Simon and Garfunkel, The Righteous Brothers, The Mamas and the Papas, and the Monkees made Rosalie move to every beat.

Movies began to fill the expanse of the window. The Graduate went by as Simon and Garfunkel sang 'Mrs. Robinson'.

'Bond, James Bond' was heard as the opening gunshot rings out. The Bond music theme is unforgettable. Mary Poppins flies by holding onto her umbrella only to be replaced by Maria from the Sound of Music.

The finale has SSgt Barry Sadler singing The Ballad of the Green Berets as scenes from Viet Nam filled the inside of the cyclone. Demonstrators across the country are seen. So many fighting men were shunned by the people back home. The government was not listening to the people. Anti-establishment youths became Hippies showing up across the country culminating with the famous concert at Woodstock.

More assassinations rang out with two high profile people, Martin Luther King, Jr. and Robert Kennedy depicted. The once highly regarded ideals of the early 1960s turned bitter overnight. Even knowing what future events were to come these images intensified Rosie's sadness she experienced from that decade.

ONLY A FEW REMAIN

Christine was sitting comfortably in her chair as she focused on her new subject. Tuned in, she listened to a ten-year-old questioning her own conduct.

"I don't know why Father Alfred is so nice to me. I am so much of a nuisance. He does his best to guide me. I guess I'm just too much of a hellion. Today I went to the chapel and sang as loud as I could. I didn't think anyone would hear me. I forgot that the nuns have super hearing. Instead of reprimanding me they actually said they enjoyed hearing me sing. Go figure."

"One time my friend and I found the sister's secret stash of goodies in a closet next to the kitchen. We were enjoying the treats so much we didn't notice she had come into the room. Would you believe she actually stuffed us into that closet and made us stay there in the dark for what seemed an eternity?"

"There was this silly boy who was trying to impress us girls. He accidently swallowed a penny. Boy, you should have seen the nuns. They came over so quickly and turned him upside down and tried to shake it out of him. We couldn't help but laugh."

"After that incident whenever he tried to show off or annoy us we would tell the nuns he swallowed something. They would go into shakedown mode and we would sit back and watch the fun as they tried to get whatever they thought he swallowed out of him."

"I thought this place would be a terrible place to live. In fact, it isn't too bad at all. Unfortunately, I will have to go back home soon. I won't miss going to the public school down the street though. Whenever something goes wrong at school the kids from the orphanage were usually blamed."

Christine teleported herself into another child's thoughts. She was a guardian of the state. She started out in the orphanage before being placed in foster care. The family didn't work out and she was returned to St. Ann's.

"As I sit here at Newman House I reflect back at the past years. So many little things happened that really don't need to be said. They are those little memories that remind me why I work hard at being a good person."

"Once I fell off the swings at the old playgrounds landing hard enough on the pavement to bruise myself pretty good. Another time I was running when I should have been walking and skinned my knees. I guess you could say I'm a bit of a klutz."

"The worse damage came when I was riding a bike around the swimming pool. I was drinking a bottle of tonic (soda) as I maneuvered my way through the course. I was suddenly taken aback by this cute boy. His distraction caused me to lose control of my vehicle. I landed hard on the path and the bottle broke cutting into my arm. It was off to the hospital to get a bunch of stitches."

"No matter what happened, a little scrape or a major fall, the nuns were right there to take care of us. Their kindness was there when it really counted. I endeavor to follow their example the rest of my life."

Christine jumped to a twelve-year-old boy. He was on his way across town to a boys' facility since older boys were not allowed to stay at St. Ann's. He reflected on memories of his stay from the past years.

"I guess the big news was back in 1964 when that kid got himself lost in the woods. He was about seven-years-old when it happened. Just before diner time the nuns noticed he wasn't anywhere to be found. They did a quick search of the buildings before calling out the authorities."

Lost Boy, 7, Is Found Safe

"Before we knew it there were nearly a thousand people from across Worcester County looking for him. Even the National Guard showed up with these huge search lights. They finally found him safe and sound sometime after ten pm in the woods below the baseball fields. That's where the nuns taught us how to play baseball and football. They were pretty good athletes and we did learn a lot from them."

"There is so much to remember. There were those day trips, the pool in the summer, and the kitchen that could make enough food to feed an army. Since there weren't many kids staying at the orphanage we each had our own sink in the bathroom. The open showers echoed with our voices. The near vacant building seemed to create an echo when we spoke. Sunday Masses in the chapel and those cool haircuts! The Worcester Telegram took pictures of us at the Red Sox game we went to. There was plenty of things to do and kids to play with. I'll miss my new friends. Maybe we'll meet again, someday."

DECISIONS MADE AND CARRIED OUT

We leave Christine as she breaks her connection with the children of St. Ann's Past. The starship I am on has jumped forward in time and shows a new change to St. Ann's Orphanage. Radiating across the screen are numerous announcements. The first one rings true to many children from St. Ann's Orphanage. One topic they are all too familiar with, name change.

The announcement reads: **May 16, 1966** - The name **St. Ann's French Canadian Orphanage** has been changed to **Mount St. Ann** eliminating the "orphanage" tag. The institution is no longer considered an "orphanage" but a temporary residence for children from troubled homes. School classes will no longer be held at this establishment and the sisters and youngsters will no longer converse in French.

More Headlines follow:

Dec. 31, 1966 - Sister Marie Doucette, S.G.M., Superior, told the board in her report that **as of Dec. 31, 1966, 10,727 children and infants had been cared for** during the tenure of the Grey Nuns - the Sisters of Charity of Montreal. Plans are being made to tear down the old orphanage buildings that had been added over the years, and parts dating to its founding 75 years ago. Stating, "These changes keep in line with the services now provided by the home which gives mainly temporary care to children on their way to foster homes or other placements. Mount St. Ann is a non-sectarian agency and receives support of Community Services, in addition to private benefactors and the Catholic diocese."

March 26, 1967 - Worcester Sunday Telegram Picture Caption - Mount St. Ann, the former St. Anne's Orphanage at 133

Granite Street, which is scheduled to be razed. Age brought with it unsafe and unhealthy conditions. In effect, the building had been condemned.

April 8, 1967 - Before Mount St. Ann is razed there will be a Final Reunion for all the former residents of St. Anne's Orphanage on 133 Granite Street. A tour of the buildings and a dinner will make the event special for all those who wish to rekindle memories of their childhood.

I turned to Sky and said. "You know, back in 1941 at the fiftieth anniversary it took a whole week to celebrate. Now, here they are in 1967. It only takes one day to celebrate and it's done with no pomp and circumstance. What a shame. I guess it's hard to say good-bye."

Next posted on the monitor:

August 1968 - The 25 children living at Mount St. Ann, Formerly, St. Ann's Orphanage are being moved to the Newman House of the Roman Catholic Diocese of Worcester at 201 Salisbury Street. Most of the home's staff will be moved to a smaller diocese owned building on Ward Street. Soon will follow the demolition of all the buildings and grounds located at 133 Granite Street. This is in preparation for five cottages (which could accommodate a total of 40 children) and an administration building, a one-story brick structure all costing $900,000. Two cottages will be for boys ages 5-12, two for girls ages 5-12, and the last for girls ages 13-16. The administration building will house a chapel, an assembly hall, counselling offices and kitchen facilities. Groundbreaking is set for Oct. 16, 1968.

186

INNOCENCE BEGUILED

Sky informs Christine that she is about to make a final connection with a nine-year old who is retelling stories from the weeks prior to moving to the temporary home on Salisbury Street. Her mind interweaves with the young girl who appears to be enjoying her narration. Cathy is sitting with two of the newest girls who have moved with the rest of the children to the Newman House.

"Just this past summer, that's 1968 for you who don't know what year this is, we were taken on a tour of this grand manor. As you can see, it is a big white house they call the Newman House. Only a few dozen people could fit in the house. Since there were about a dozen boys and a dozen girls plus the bunch of nuns it fit perfectly."

"As we entered the house we were greeted to a large bannister staircase. I'm sure you will each get your turn to clean and shine it. We were shuffled throughout the house in the usual orderly fashion. One room we walked into will be embedded in my mind forever. What was to become the junior girls' bathroom had a boys' wall urinal. At that time, we had no clue what it was. Before we could question what that mysterious thing was the nuns quickly ushered us out of there."

"During this past summer we had a lot of fun. We took a day trip to a camp site beside a pond. Father Alfred gave a small mass of sorts before the festivities started. Most of the nuns, all the kids and some of the kids' relatives were there to enjoy the day. We played games, splashed in the pond and ate lots of fun food. That is one day I will never forget."

"If you two girls are good you might come with us to some of the places they have planned for us this fall and winter. I think they are planning on taking us to the ballet or what they call the Nutcracker Suite. I think they are taking us swimming to an indoor swimming pool and to do other things at the Assumption College. Let's not forget a visit with Santa Claus come Christmas time."

"The nuns were given permission to modernize the habits they wear. They used to wear these heavy, dark gray things. They were so hot in the summertime you could see the poor sisters sweating. Some of the girls believed that the nuns had their heads shaved. One day one of the girls asked a young nun. She smiled and pulled out a lock of beautiful blonde hair for us to see. Well, soon after that the nuns started wearing these real nice looking habits and head covers. They look so much better now and a lot less scary."

"We used to have one of the sisters play the guitar and sing at the folk masses. Do you know that at one time I wanted to be a nun? Of course you don't. I even talked with Father Alfred about it. He told me that if it was all about the habit, then I really didn't have the calling. I didn't mind. The sister didn't have the calling either. She left the Order to get married and have children of her own. Mass was never the same. She comes by and visits when something special is happening."

"Now, before we all go off to bed, let me tell you the scariest story you've ever heard. It is about the insane nun who used to live in the old buildings. This was just before we moved here to Salisbury Street. I believe there were about a dozen girls and another dozen boys still residing at the buildings on Granite Street. So the big old place was very empty. Emptier and scarier than ever."

"One afternoon myself and two other girls decided to find the room that held the insane nun, to make sure she hadn't escaped. We had heard the story from a couple very reliable senior girls so her existence was certain. They were so wonderful to share their terrifying secret with us. After all we were just lowly junior girls eight and nine years old. They would trust us, but… we were never to tell a living sole."

"We followed their instructions to the letter. We snuck up the hallway past the boy's area and went up a steep set of stairs. Then down a long dark hallway. We could almost hear her screaming, insanely of course. It was getting dark out and the old place looked scarier than usual. Couple that with our wild childhood imaginations and you have it. We were terrified! We went into an area we were not allowed to go, ever! Our mentors, those senior girls, needed us to go and make sure the crazy nun was still chained to her bed."

"Finally, we came to this room at the end of the hall. We mustered up the nerve to open the big heavy door that blocked our way into the room. It screeched like a murder victim as we slowly opened it. We then double dog dared each other to go inside. Then we relied on Eeny, meeny, miny, moe to pick on who would go inside first. We were about to see this mad, crazy, insane nun."

"Her name was Sister Vicieux, but all the kids called her Sister Vicious. She had been so mean to all the kids. Her hatred for the stupid younger girls finally drove her crazy. At least that's how it was told by the senior girls. One night she went off her rocker and tried killing the junior girls while they slept in their dormitory beds."

"I don't recall which one of us went in first. I think our imaginations took over our fears as we slowly crept into the eerie room one by one. In the far reaches of the room we believed we could see a butcher block with a knife sticking out of it. We swear we could see blood spattered about the room."

"As our eyes got accustomed to the darkness we saw a chair, no a wheel chair, with someone sitting in it. The chair turned to reveal someone in a nun's disheveled habit. We didn't see any chains as the person spoke in a raspy old woman's voice. 'What are you children doing here? Would you like to come in and join me in some 'Little Girl Stew?' A hideous cackling laugh emanated from her as she maneuvered her wheelchair towards us."

"Well, you've never seen three little girls move so fast. We screamed all the way through the building yelling, 'She's escaped! The crazy nun isn't chained and is coming to get us! She's going to kill us!' We didn't stop until we found the good nuns who we knew would protect us. Breathlessly we told them the grim news. We were not met with a hero's welcome. Instead, we were reprimanded for being in the forbidden areas of the building."

"I remember seeing the senior girls washing dishes in the kitchen for many days after that. I tried to say hi to them, but they only smirked at us. They were no longer our best buddies. From that night on I slept curled up in a ball at the end of my bed. That way the vicious Sister Vicieux wouldn't be able to find me and kill me for disturbing her. I was so happy when we moved here to Salisbury Street."

"Well girls, that should keep your imagination churning tonight. Go brush your teeth and get yourselves ready for bed."

Christine found herself pulling away from Cathy's mind, returning in body and spirit to her soft chair on the Tardis.

Chapter 10

Return to the Grotto

THROUGH HEAVEN'S GATE

The wind subsided and the tornado dissipated causing Rosalie's house to fall downward. Sky gently placed it in the open field next to the grotto. She disembarked her house and witnesses a grand procession of children making their way up the steps of the grotto. Christine's Tardis landed on the sidewalk of Granite Street. She bade Sky farewell before exiting to see the same glorious site. I said the words "Beam me down, Sky" and was instantly transported from the spaceship's bridge onto the street next to Rosalie and Christine.

We looked at each other and felt a converging sensation. Somehow, we saw what each of us had separately encountered. "Did you guys just feel that?" asked Rosalie. We both nodded. "That's wonderful. I know exactly what you guys just experienced. I thought I was going to miss all that newly found wisdom."

Christine interrupted. "Look at that. We're back at the grotto. This isn't the same procession we saw back in the 50s. There must be thousands of children here. Ghost Children!"

"You're right." I said. "There has to be thousands of kids here, they must be the Ghosts of St. Ann's Past. Oh my, this is the real deal. Look up there." We were not witnessing the staged recreation of the Crowning of Mary. We were witnessing much more. To our amazement we were looking at something most Holy, the Gates of Heaven. We could see clouds engulfing the Gates. Cherubs and angels were assisting the procession of children, up to and through the gates of heaven.

Rosalie yelled. "Look, I see Otto and Violette waving to us." We waved back. "Au revoir, mes Amis." Hundreds, no thousands of children continued to pass through the gates. They made one last gaze upon their childhood home before disappearing into the glorious expanse of heaven.

Artwork by Soher Jesus Silva-Alvarado

Thru the crowds of children, we could see three figures coming toward us. It was Robert, Thomasina and Donald. "Hello," said Robert. "We wanted to say thank you for letting us guide you through this journey. We are going home to Jesus and will finally be at peace."

Thomasina said. "You are witnesses to our ascension into heaven because you took the time to research the history and gather our stories so it will be remembered forever."

Donald said. "People will read these stories and remember the beauty here at St. Ann's Orphanage. They will remember all the children along with the good and the bad. You made this most special event happen for us and we are forever grateful. We will meet you again at heaven's gate and we will all be together again."

We thanked them for the wonderful experience we had and their help along the way. We gave each other hugs and the children turned and headed up the stairs to their new beginning.

Christine noticed someone waving to us from the top of the stairs. "I believe I see St. Bernadette with another Grey Nun. She's calling us to meet with them."

We acknowledged her request and made our way to the top of the stairs all the while bidding adieu to the children filing two by two into the gaping orifice. We are greeted by Saint Bernadette. "It is so nice to see you again. Has your journey been a good one for you?"

I said as graciously as possible. "It has been much more than a journey or an experience. Enlightening gives it more credence. But in all reality, there are no words to describe what we have encountered. We all thank you so much for giving us this incredible opportunity to witness such a spectacle."

"Oh dear, pardonnez-moi. I have not introduced you to the last encounter of your journey. May I present the person who started all of this, Madame Marie-Marguerite d'Youville."

After our short pleasantries Rosalie could no longer control herself. With her hands on her chest Rosalie says "Oh my God! I'm totally in shock. I can't believe that this dream of mine to actually meet you has come true. I so want to hug you."

"We have been so blessed to have had this journey and to have seen for ourselves the trials and tribulations of the sisters and children of St. Ann's Orphanage. We thank you for giving your life to help and care for so many people. I am truly honored to be standing here with you. S'il vous plaît, permettez-moi de vous appelez mon amie! Please let me call you my friend!"

Marguerite responded. "Merci, mon amie. As you know my life was dedicated to the sick and needy people of Montreal. The establishment of the Grey Nuns has indeed helped ease the pain and suffering of so many people. They have spread their wings across the globe serving so many needy souls. I am so honored that so many people look upon me with such favor."

The last of the children made their way into the fold above the statue of Mary as I ask. "Why is it that we meet here today? I feel that something very important is about to unfold. Is something about to happen that has cause for calling all the passed souls to heaven on such a beautiful day?"

With my final word an ear shattering crash comes from across Granite Street. We all turned to view the final destruction of the St. Ann's French Canadian Orphanage. We now realize it is the summer of 1968 and the childhood home of so many children is about to come to an end.

EVERY ENDING HAS A NEW BEGINNING

We stand in reverence to the razing of our childhood home. We see the side landings tumble down with the slight touch of a mighty machine. The original wooden building had been standing proud at the edge of Granite Street since 1893. It now succumbs to the destructive force of heavy metal. The bridge that bonded the family home with a tight grip since 1923 receives one hard blow before its cord is severed, disintegrating the unity of the two. Bricks may be strong, but aging has weakened the bonds that held them together making easy the work of the destructors.

The last to see its demise is the house that Bowman built. It housed all the sisters since 1904. We shed a tear or two as the last façade falls with a deafening sound. As the large machines pull over to one side and shut down we can hear the moaning and creaking of this once glorious place. The sounds dissipate as we hear the last timber settle quietly into final rest.

We turn to each other with tears in our eyes. Marguerite speaks in a soft, yet assuring voice. "Now my children, don't you fret. You know that with every ending there is a new beginning. We know that it is not over. Soon St. Ann's Orphanage will live on in the name of Mount St. Ann. There are still hundreds of children and adults who will benefit from her rebirth."

Saint Marguerite begged. "Please kneel with me as I say a final prayer for all those children who have left us today. We will also pray for all those children, like yourselves who someday will pass through these same gates to be united with all your brothers and sisters from St. Ann's Orphanage."

We knelt beside our two beloved saints. Marguerite looked into the Gates of Heaven and prayed: "Father in Heaven, we beseech you take to your side those gifts we have presented to you today and the souls of those who still are of this earth who will someday join their brothers and sisters of St. Ann's French Canadian Orphanage. We are and will always be your humble servants. In the name of the Father, the Son and the Holy Spirit."

We all replied in unison. "AMEN."

Before we could collect our senses Saint Marguerite and Saint Bernadette stood up and passed through Heaven's Gate. I yelled out, "Bernadette, please don't go! I still have so many questions to ask you!".

"My dream had abruptly concluded. My calling out in such a panic not only woke me but both of you."

Chapter 11

Back Home

INTERPRETATION

With a fresh cup of tea and a quick run to our nearby Dunkin Donuts for coffee and a dozen Boston Cream donuts we returned to the table for some discussion.

I started out by asking Rosie and Chris what they thought about my dream. Chris' response, "Inspiring. We should write a book." Rosie said. "Your dream was amazing! Very intriguing. How did you come up with all this stuff? Chris is right. We should write a book about 'The Ghosts of St. Ann's Past."

"I really don't know, Rosie. Maybe it was all that digging into St. Anne's history for these past few months that prompted it. Somehow my brain was working overtime trying to put it all in context. I guess it put the information into chronological story form and presented it to me in the dream. All I can say is it has put the entire lifespan of St. Anne's in full perspective."

Rosie said. "It's so wonderful how St. Bernadette became the focal point of the story. I bet most people who visit the grotto think that petite statue is just a little girl praying to Mary. As we know she is St. Bernadette, the young girl who had eighteen visionary contacts with Mary. I see your dream had eighteen holy apparitions. I loved meeting Violette and Otto. They were so nice. It's so sad they had such tragic endings. Talking with Marguerite d'Youville, the founder of the Grey Nuns brought it all together."

Christine added. "You know if you write a book people will ask you if it is all real or just plain made up."

I reacted. "It's not a secret that we collected a lot of stuff from blogs, emails, newspapers and historical archives. All I can say is that the book would be based on researched historical facts and recalled memories of former residents of St. Anne's. Historical information we found in different newspapers wasn't quite exact. We had to rely on different newspaper articles and archived documents to come up with conclusive dates and information. I believe our historical timeline is now the most accurate."

Chris asked. "There are topics you touched upon in your dream that may be considered controversial. What about the allegations of abuse and exploitation of the children?"

"As we are well aware abuse has been a part of society for hundreds of years. When we were growing up I knew kids who were severely punished by their fathers. I also knew kids who got away with a lot of things and did not get any punishment."

"As we did our research I compared stories told about St. Anne's and other orphanages. If I were to rank these places from one to ten, with ten the worst, St. Anne's would be a two or three.

200

Believe me, some of the places I read about were down right evil. Some orphanages, usually run by men, were nothing but places that provided these young girls to pleasure seekers. I believe these were not in the United States, but anything is possible."

"There was an episode on Murdock Mysteries, a Canadian TV series set at the turn of the twentieth century that did an excellent job showing the exploitation of orphaned children. Girls and boys were first brought to local orphanages. These were more or less weigh stations where the girls would be matched up with adoptive parents. On the other hand, the boys would end up in work houses. Each physically abused in different ways. High society at its worst"

"So, within the stories at St. Anne's I found various degrees of abuse. Physical abuse consisted of spanking, slapping or striking a child with an object. Mental or psychological abuse consisted of making a child feel useless, unworthy, embarrassed or humiliated. Although memories have alleged the possibility, no one has come out to say there was sexual abuse. On the contrary, people who did remark on this subject stated they did not experience, see or hear of this happening."

"Some kids stated they were punished severely while others had minimal, if any punishment at all. I can't give you a reason for the wide discrepancy. I can only hypothesize that whatever abuse they had before and after their internment at the orphanage may have been a benchmark to the severity of what they received at St. Anne's."

"I can say that most of the stories have a common ending. The former residents of St. Anne's Orphanage went through their lives with issues relating to their specific childhood experiences.

Even with help from family, friends and clergy they lived their lives with the insecurities of their youth. That was and is the cross we all bear."

HISTORICALLY SPEAKING

"Alright," said Rosie. "Enough with the depressing stuff. What about St. Anne's and Worcester, Massachusetts?"

"As you know Rosie, between the book and our Facebook page we can now get a better look at the history of St. Anne's Orphanage. We both know it when I say we had an uphill battle on our hands when we started. As we searched we could not find anything on St. Anne's. People posted on numerous blogs the same concerns about the lack of information. We found very little at the Worcester Library. The newspapers are only on microfilm, making random searches virtually impossible."

"Most of the places you expect to get information from had nothing. We searched historical websites in the Worcester area. They did not provide anything about St. Anne's. We searched YouTube videos and found historical photos and such of Worcester. None mentioned or showed photos of St. Anne's Orphanage. Even the Worcester Historical Museum doesn't have anything. It's almost as if St. Anne's Orphanage was a disease that no one wanted to know or speak about."

"It took three trips to Worcester and many phone calls before finding some help. We contacted the Catholic Charities of Worcester County. With some luck we were able to connect with the keeper of the only known entry log books of St. Anne's

Orphanage. Other than getting our own personal information privacy rules denied us access to other information such as how far back the logs went."

Christine provided some input at this time. "On one of our trips Joe and I stopped in at the Catholic Free Press. The people were very friendly and obliging to us. They brought out a folder they had and allowed us to copy its contents. Photographs with names written on the back, newspaper articles and announcements filled the file. They even had an official Dedication Program from the 1951 Playground Ceremony. We now use a copy of the St. Anne's Orphanage aerial photo for our Facebook Cover. We went home very happy that day."

I continued. "That's right Chris. I also think that day was a big reason for our continued efforts. So many people who had been touched by St. Anne's over the years needed to get a sense of what their youth at St. Anne's Orphanage was about. Since we started our Facebook page in May, 2015 many people have visited it. Some were looking for information about family members and others provided us with stories and photos."

"It's been almost a year and we have received so many wonderful, heartfelt stories and great pictures. Some of them go back to the beginning of St. Anne's. I even have the 1900, 1910 and 1920 U.S. census PDFs for St. Ann's French Canadian Orphanage. Hundreds of names are listed. I hope to get more."

MOUNT ST. ANN

Rosie spoke next. "You know Joe, there's a whole new story that could be told as a continuation of your story. The demolition of St. Anne's closed the book on her past but opened a new chapter in modern childcare."

"The 1960s brought about massive changes. Decreasing the population and changing the name to Mount St. Ann were just the beginning. Once it was incorporated into the new childcare system it was only a matter of time before the old buildings were razed. In the summer of 1968 the buildings were closed for good and demolition began. By October they were breaking ground for the new buildings of Mount St. Ann. Less than two years after razing St. Anne's, on May 1, 1970 Mount St. Ann was officially opened."

Chris made note. "I saw many posts from former Mount St. Ann residents. They too had a lot of memories of their time during the 70s and 80s. They described the places they went to and the small gatherings they had. With forty kids it was easier for them to know the names of the others living there."

"We have so many pictures posted on our Facebook page of the children and buildings from that time. Each time someone sees a picture they comment about it. The new pool provided so much fun time during the summers. Going to different venues was a lot of fun too. It was like a big, happy family when they were together. I'm sure it helped them forget the troubles they had with their own families."

I said. "I hope someday, someone who had the Mount St. Ann experience takes time to write a book. It would surely be the sequel to our story."

GOODBYE, FOR NOW

"It's only fair I mention that after the close of Mount St. Ann in 1983 and departure of the Grey Nuns in 1987, it too went through many changes. It has slowly dissipated into the ruins we see today. Our visit to the site in the fall of 2015 showed a shell of its former self. The pool was no longer. It was now just a filled in parking lot. Only two of the buildings were still in use. They provided single needy mothers a refuge for themselves and their children."

"The buildings of Mount St. Ann are now facing the same fate as our beloved buildings of St. Anne's Orphanage. 2016 will close the book on the 125 years since the inception of this great historical site. One hundred fifty acres of beautiful farmland dwindled down to a pile of rubble sold off to different entities."

With tears in our eyes we bow our heads and think about our personal thoughts and memories from our residency at this institution. We would like to thank this grand place for being there when we needed sanctuary. Good, bad or indifferent it served a purpose in all our lives. Our paths went in many directions but eventually we will all meet again with the knowledge that each of us have a common connection.

Jusqu'a la prochaine fois qu'on nous soyons ensemble, garder toujours votre sourrire. (Until we meet again, keep smiling.)

Fini

ROSIE WANTS TO SAY A LITTLE MORE!

Wow, how do I thank everyone who has helped in this journey of ours in one word? I just can't. I do need to thank the most important person for me, my mom. For us, we would not be on this wonderful journey that has opened our eyes and brought us so much joy and understanding if it were not for my mom.

My mom had no choice in placing us with the Grey Nuns. She believed we would be safe and cared for and not harmed. Things were not always happy at the Orphanage, but I was taught not to judge a book by its cover (oh the wonders you will find by going beyond the cover and reading). We truly were in a better place and I have finally realized this in learning more about the Grey Nuns when we visited them in Canada.

I can only say thank you to my brother Joe who believed in me. Together we found out that my recurring dreams were a real part of my past youth. You were there with me, and we determined that God was sending us on a mission.

I know how hard it was for Joe to believe what I remembered until his own memories were confirmed when we went on our first mission to the Worcester Public Library. He just listened and helped me search and read all we could find about St. Anne's Orphanage.

With the help of a lot of the residents of St. Anne's we found out more than we bargained for. Many told of their stories while at St. Anne's. Some even sent photos, and newspaper articles. Their help made us understand this was more than about us. The memories started to flood our thoughts as we remembered more and more.

We put all of the children's memories, the history of St. Anne's Orphanage and historical information together. At first I did not think I could do this but my friends told me I could do anything. I just needed to believe in myself. Joe and I took a leap of faith and wrote this story.

Along this journey I have learned that I am worthy of God's love. I put God to the side for a long time thinking he really did not care for the likes of me. All this time I had not realized that God's love was always there for the taking. All I needed was to believe and trust in him.

I have read and learned a lot about Saint Marguerite. I have come to truly admire her. She started through her love of God to establish the order of the Grey Nuns. With her kindness and love she helped so many people survive and through her own tragedies gave the little she had. She provided food and clothing with a warm place to sleep, and lots of love.

Reading about Saint Bernadette's plight was also a sad but wonderful story. Her love of Jesus and how she believed when no one else wanted to believe her. She kept her faith strong while being mocked by the crowds when she talked to Mary during her eighteen visions. How more awesome could that be?

We have heard so many stories from the children of St. Anne's Orphanage. The most intriguing one was them telling us that they could not understand why they had to be there and endure what happened to them. Joe and I fully understood their plight.

Laying in our small beds we would look up at the ceiling and hear the faint crying of the children's loneliness. Even today I wake up and think of the sadness we felt when we lived there. For the longest time I felt it was my fault we were in the orphanage. I will never forget the good and bad memories of the past.

Sourire souvent, être gentil, rire, rêver grand et de l'amour! Un grand merci à tous ceux qui ont contribué à faire de ce voyage arrive. (Smile often, be kind, laugh, dream big and love! Many thanks to all that helped to make this journey happen.)

We are all SURVIVORS of the Ghosts of St. Ann's Past!

Rick Blackburn, you are the love of my life. Thank you for letting me see that my story needed to be told. I wish you could have been on this journey with me. I believe you are smiling down on me from heaven and would be proud of what I have accomplished. I miss and will love you forever.

HISTORICAL TIMELINE

The History of St. Ann's French Canadian Orphanage of Worcester

Edited May 16, 2016

Here is St. Ann's French Canadian Orphanage's historical timeline we were able to collect and collate from local newspaper articles and documents provided to us from different organizations including; the Worcester Public Library, the Catholic Free Press, the Community Chest Member, the Worcester Telegram, the Worcester Telegraph, the Boston Globe and the Sœurs de la Charité de Montréal «Sœurs Grises» Maison de Mère d'Youville, Sœurs Grises Archives de Montreal – Better known as The Sisters of Charity of Montreal, "Grey Nuns" house of mother d'Youville, Grey Nuns Archives of Montreal.

St. Ann's French Canadian Orphanage
Also known as:
The French-Canadian Orphanage of Worcester
St. Anne's Orphanage
St. Ann's Orphanage
Mount St. Ann
Catholic Charities Worcester County Youville House

The Grey Nuns were formally called the Sisters of Charity of Montreal
The non-sectarian home was a Golden Rule Agency teaching and guiding their charges the golden rule. (The Golden Rule - The common English phrasing is "Do unto others as you would have them do unto you.")

The orphanage initially served the Franco-American community, housing as much as 250 children at one time who had no parents, or whose parents were unable to care for them, or parents who just abandoned them. In the early days, it was a place where children came to live until they became adults. As time

209

passed the reasons also changed to include finding adoptive homes. Illness of a parent meant temporary boarding and possible return to the family. However, by the 1970's most of the children at Mount St. Ann were temporary residents who came from troubled homes where some other domestic problem meant they must be relocated. After a short time, they were returned to their homes or placed in foster homes. Eventually, the last residents were families needing shelter. Then, the Youville House provided shelter for the homeless and people with addiction. Lastly, it served as a home for single mothers with children in need of care.

Aug. 8 – 1889 - Father Brouillet, curate of Notre Dame Church, rented a house at 96 Southgate Street to serve as an orphanage and temporary school for about 25-30 boys and girls and a home for the elderly. He was concerned about the plight of children left parentless and the elderly left to fend for themselves in those poverty-ridden times. It was then called the French-Canadian Orphanage of Worcester and run by a few young ladies from the Third Order of St. Francis.

1889 - Sister Victoria Bessette, at the age of eight, was one of four sisters who were left
Motherless. They became one of the first children to go to the French-Canadian Orphanage of Worcester, which was also a boarding school. She was also the first resident of St. Anne's Orphanage to become a Grey Nun.

Jan. 31, 1891 – After disagreements with the Third Order of St. Francis, Father Broulette invited the Grey Nuns of Montreal (The Sisters of Charity) to take charge of the orphanage. Reverend Mother Deschamps, Superior General, sent some sisters to take on this task. Sisters Piche, La Point and George have been mentioned in articles. They assumed the responsibility of the orphan home at 96 Southgate Street and the children left parentless in those poverty ridden times. The population of the orphans and deserted children quickly grew to 50. It was up to these sisters to take complete care of their charges. That meant feeding, clothing, caring, and teaching them. It also meant that the sisters had to find ways to raise funds for the clothing, food and fuel by going house

210

to house to solicit funds, etc. When the sisters put the children to bed they washed the few cloths they had. The property was neither sanitary nor well-built. It was so damp after a heavy rain, they sloshed about in rubber boots. They had to scrub the floors before the children could play on them. They were utterly dependent on the goodness of others. Many a day the children would want for food.

1891 - The Society of Benefactors was organized. Within a year they would support the building of a new orphanage high on the hills of Granite Street for a cost of $15,000.

1891 - The order of Grey Nuns of Montreal (The Sisters of Charity) purchased Ellsworth Farm, comprising about 150 acres (confirmed by Worcester Map of 1896) located at 133 Granite Street. On this farm was a house and a barn. Building of a four-story wooden structure started immediately. It was typical to the style of other institutions of that period. It contained a school and was a complete and modern entity for its day.

1891 – In addition to the three founding sisters, 10 more missionaries were later sent to help support the French-Canadian Orphanage of Worcester. Sisters Hedwidge, Lapoint, Kegle, Waters, Menard, Ursula, Damascus, McKenzie, St. Louis Gomzague and Lynch.

February 27, 1892 - An Agreement of Association was signed and notarized and the St. Ann's French Canadian Orphanage was incorporated. (In honor of the Superior, Reverend Mother Anna Piche.)

January 3, 1893 - The Grey Nuns, led by Mother Anna Piche, Superior, moved into the new simple four-story wooden structure. Fourteen acres of the massive site were utilized for farming. They were still very poor and everyone worked the farm, tended the animals, made cloths, etc. to make ends meet. Yet, no one was turned away. St. Anne's Orphanage eventually prospered and grew. The farm was worked by the children, Grey Nuns and hired hands. It produced vegetables, poultry, dairy products and pigs to feed the children, whose numbers would later grow to more than 250.

1904 - Mrs. Bowman Wood, a local widower, was so moved by the work of the children and the Grey Nuns that she gifted her home to them with the stipulation it be used for religious purposes only. The house was moved and attached to the 4-story wooden structure. A picture from 1893 shows the new 4-story white building standing alone and a 1904 picture shows the combined house and 4-story white building. Confirming this action was a 1963 newspaper article that stated "The house was then added to the main building and served as a dormitory for the sisters." The Grey nuns also build their own chapel in the newly attached building.

1920 - The barn burned down, causing a loss of $16,500 and stored documents. The barn was quickly rebuilt since it was an integral part of the farm. It meant more house to house solicitations to keep up with the high costs.

1922 – The Orphans Friend Society, known in French as "Ami de l'Orphelin" was established. Five Catholic parishes in Worcester wholly or partly composed of French people were represented in this society, the membership of which included men and women.

1923 – The Board of Public Safety declared the top floor of the 4-story wooden structure unsafe as a residence in which to house the children. $160,000 was borrowed from a local bank and a large four story brick dormitory that conformed to fire regulations was built behind the older wooden buildings with accommodations for up to 250 children. A bridge corridor connected the new and older buildings. The older buildings continued to be used as a school, chapel, kitchen and dining room. The orphanage became a member of the Community Chest and started receiving funds through the annual Golden Rule Drive and Red Feather drive.

If it were not for these benefactors St. Anne's Orphanage might have had to close their doors to all those children in need.

August 30, 1936 - Sister Clara Bourgon described St. Anne's Orphanage in an article. "After 45 years St. Anne's has taken charge of nearly 7,000 children. There are about 170 children residing here. St. Anne's offers its children an unusual and excellent combination of home, school and church under its ample roof."

"We do everything which can be done for a child. When they are sick, we care for them: when they are babies we dress and feed them. As they grow older, we instruct them in school and religion. We make many of their clothes. We have warm showers for them in the basement, that they may be always clean. During the summer we have picnics, outdoor roasts. The knights of Columbus and the Elk Lodges take the children on annual picnics, and often treat the entire group to motion pictures. Occasionally friends or relatives take them, individually, for excursions. We try not only to make them good children, and healthier children, but to make them happy."

"Our youngest children now are about two years old. They call the little ones of nursery age "Rose Babies". Pink dresses with white collars are made for the girls, and trim play-suits for the little boys. The Rose Babies sleep in pink beds, in big, airy rooms, with pink curtains at the windows."

"For older girls, the beds are tinted a soft blue, still older girls find themselves in quarters slightly more mature. The children are grouped according to age, and to sex, and sleet in large rooms which accommodate about 60. The beds are set row by row across the wide area, and a protecting sister sleeps at the head of the room. Off each sleeping room is the "Infirmary," a little room where a sick of feverish child may be tended."

"There are playrooms for the tiny tots, made gay with dolls and tiny tea tables and bright colored games. Each room is given an atmosphere of home with plants growing in the rooms. There are sewing rooms next to each dormitory where the Sisters older girls make clothes for the younger ones. The girls also work on the beautiful embroideries for which St. Anne's is known. These appear in window curtains, pillow cases and piano scarfs. Pianos also play an important part there. Music instruction is not compulsory, but if a boy or girl shows a desire to learn the piano, or exhibits some real ability, both piano and singing are taught."

"There are screened-in porches on each floor and these serve as outdoor playrooms. There is also a play yard with swings and see-saws and rolling fields in which to romp. During the summer, many children so invited are permitted to visit relatives."

"The Sisters of St. Anne's are proud of their modern kitchen and of their wide, bright dining-room."

"In their own school, they are drilled in the old standbys of "readin', writin', and 'rithmetic," with geography, history and penmanship as other subjects. The Sisters serve as teachers, with the exception of one grade presided over by a Normal School graduate who besides teaching regular subjects, affords the children practice in spoken and written English. Though the Sisters speak English their native French tongue comes more easily to them, especially for writing, and while the children are taught French, they want them to be well schooled in English."

"St. Anne's is the only agency among all those supported through the Community Chest's annual Golden Rule Fund, which sponsors its own school. This corresponds to a grammar school and carries the pupils up to the sixth grade. For the seventh and eighth grade they go outside to one of the parochial schools and for high school they attend Ascension."

"Though the proper name of the orphanage is St. Anne's French Canadian Orphanage might suggest that only French children would be admitted, almost any nationality is welcome. There are Irish, Polish and Italian children in the nursery play room and in the school rooms. All children are, at this moment, in good health. They are examined every year by Dr. William E. Langlois or the department of public health and checked every week by the school nurse, Miss. Eva Harpin. Their teeth are kept in 100 per cent perfect condition by regular attendance at the dental clinic of the Providence Street Junior High School."

December 27, 1939 – A fire started in the first floor rubbish shoot and quickly spread up the shaft to the roof and mushroomed out onto the fourth floor. Fortunately, this being holiday time, most of the 200 children were visiting with family or friends. The 60 or so children still at the orphanage were in the dormitories in the brick build behind the old wooden structure. It has been reported that historical documents may have been lost during this fire but there are no supporting documents to this claim.

1941 - The orphanage observed its 50th anniversary. This is well documented in photos and local newspapers. The founder of the orphanage, Reverend Mother Anna Piche, attended celebrations, which coincided with her 80th birthday. Bishop Thomas M. O'Leary celebrated a thanksgiving mass for the nuns at St. Joseph's Church in Worcester.

1941 - L'Ami des Orphelins Society (The Friends of Orphans Society) gifted land and the **"Grotto of Our Lady of Lourdes and St. Bernadette"** to St. Anne's Orphanage. It is still located across from 133 Granite Street facing the orphanage. The grotto was once reputed to be one of the most beautiful Lourdes' shrines in New England and was a popular devotional center for Worcester Catholics.

March 29, 1942 - A circular pool with a diameter of 75 feet was built by funds raised by the Harmony Club. The pool was set on a plot 350 by 200 feet. The land was graded and shrubbery aligned the walkway. It cost more than $6,000. At the deepest point, the pool was four feet. A cement walkway, eight feet wide surrounded the pool, on which children would roller skate when there is no bathing.

March 29, 1942 – "There will always be orphans-in war and in peace-and we must take care of them." There are 224 children, many of them orphaned, at St. Anne's. The number of children has increased materially during the last few months. At present the house is filled to capacity. To feed those youngsters requires 816 loaves of bread each week. Fifty gallons of milk are required for one day. Sixteen pounds of butter are consumed each day. As yet, sugar is still plentiful and though the children use it carefully, they eat 300 pounds each week, which will be about their allotment when rationing begins. St. Anne's is health conscious and nutrition is the rule. Cod liver oil is used by the barrel. The smallest children take it readily and about three gallons are licked down each week. These items are in addition to fruit, cereals, and all the other supplies necessary for well-rounded and varied meals. "Some mothers feel burdened when they must care for three or four children." There are 224 children, many of them orphaned, at St. Anne's. The staff, sisters and older children must work together to prepare and serve meals, make or make over clothes for children, buy shoes, see that the children get to school, that they have their daily naps when they are small, and plenty of sleep for all, as well as play time and snack times.

1947 - L'Ami des Orphelins Society (The Friends of Orphans Society) celebrated their 25th Anniversary with a banquet at St. Anne's Orphanage.

Early 1951 - The provincial administration headquarters of the Grey Nuns (The Sisters of Charity) in the U.S, moved to St. Anne's Orphanage, Worcester.

1951 – The resident population at St. Anne's Orphanage was about 185: Boys ages 4-12 and Girls ages 4-16. Schooling up to the sixth grade. Then they attended either St. Joseph's Parochial School or Ascension High School. Since the establishment of the orphanage many girls entered the order.

Sept. 16, 1951 – At a large ceremony four new play fields were dedicated by the Harmony Club of Worcester. The playgrounds are located to the side and rear of the orphanage. Two play areas in back of the building are for the younger children. They are equipped with swings and game devices. Two larger playgrounds to the side of St. Anne's are for the older children. One contains a tennis and volleyball court and the other a softball and baseball diamond. The play areas were given by the Harmony Club of Worcester in honor of Mr. & Mrs. Archibald R. LeMieux, 53 Elm Street.

1950's – The type of children began to change. The true 'orphan' turned to single parent boarders, then to plain unwanted and rejected children. The farm could no longer maintain itself with pigs and chickens. To keep up with the costs St. Anne's gladly took in these boarders for a fee. The sisters felt their care would be preferable to the home situation.

1957 – Many discussions were held about institutions like St. Anne's. From, "The institution is a panacea." To, "The institution is a monster." To the middle-ground, "It is useful in certain circumstances." A survey of agencies in Worcester recommended that the administration "must move to transform St. Ann's into an institution in which both charity and sound concepts of child care are present."

1959 – The Director of Catholic Charities, the Reverend Timothy J. Harrington, directed a change in the emphasis of the orphanage. New Concepts and approaches in child care were implemented. This meant changing from a non-selective policy to a selective policy. As a result, the number of children was sharply reduced. This was a milestone in that it re-focused the total program of St. Anne's Orphanage. The sisters were educated in the institutional child-care approach.

May 28, 1963 – A picture caption in a Worcester newspaper on Tuesday, May 28, 1963 - Page 27 stated that the "Unsafe and unhealthy conditions will force the wrecking soon of St. Anne's Orphanage's main building, outlined in the picture. The barns, included in the outline, are already being torn down." (See posted Clippings). The main building presently houses the kitchen and dining areas, a temporary chapel, and the administration operation of St. Anne's.

The out buildings were demolished at that time, but the main building remained for another 5 years as it would be needed a bit longer.

1963 - With the advent of foster home care replacing the orphanage, its old walls had seen a large decrease in youngsters who rapidly came and went. Rev. Msgr. Timothy J. Harrington, director of Catholic Charities, said the building would be torn down because age had brought with it unsafe and unhealthy conditions. In effect, the building had been condemned. The land was to be landscaped. Living quarters for the children, who were at St. Anne's then and afterward, was set up in the masonry building hidden from view by the wooden structure that bordered the street.

The brick building, in the past, contained classrooms and a large dormitory. This building was completely renovated so that the children would have a homelike atmosphere in which to live. It accommodated approximately 52 children. A wing was added to this building for a new boiler and janitorial services.

Once a place where children came to live until they became adults, unless they were fortunate enough to be adopted the orphanage, became a temporary shelter for children coming from their own homes or hospitals and going into foster homes while adoptive parents waited eagerly to take them home.

During the 1960's the orphanage served not only this purpose but as emergency quarters for children who needed shelter. The shelter of the orphanage was extended to 10 Cuban children who had been sent to this country for safety by their parents who remained in Cuba. The Cuban children eventually found temporary homes in the Worcester community.

The orphanage introduced a new teen program. Bishop Flanagan told the Orphanage Lay Advisory Board that the program was one of a few in the New England area and unique in that it was a separate, self-contained unit at the home.

December 21, 1963 - A steam pipe located above the boiler and too close to the ceiling created a fire in the furnace room of the brick building. The fire soon spread to a first floor room in the rear of the building destroying Christmas Gifts for the 37 children presently living there.

May 16, 1966 - The name **St. Anne's Orphanage** was changed **to Mount St. Ann** to eliminate the "orphanage" tag. The institution is no longer an "orphanage" but a temporary residence for children from troubled homes. Even the children resented the term 'orphanage' resulting in behavior problems. Classes were no longer held in the building and the sisters and youngsters no longer conversed in French.

Dec. 31, 1966 - Sister Marie Doucette, S.G.M., Superior, told the board in her report that **as of Dec. 31, 1966, 10,727 children and infants had been cared for**, operated by the Grey Nuns - the Sisters of Charity of Montreal. Plans were made to tear down the

218

old orphanage buildings that had been added over the years, and parts dating to its founding 75 years ago. Stating, "These changes keep in line with the services now provided by the home which gives mainly temporary care to children on their way to foster homes or other placements. Mount St. Ann is a non-sectarian agency and receives support of Community Services, in addition to private benefactors and the Catholic diocese."

1967 - Worcester Sunday Telegram March 26, 1967 page 22A
Picture Caption - Mount St. Ann, the former St. Anne's Orphanage on Granite Street, which is scheduled to be razed.
Note: Age brought with it unsafe and unhealthy conditions. In effect, the buildings had been condemned.
Note: The picture shown in the newspaper article was the building originally scheduled to be razed in 1963. It lasted for another 5 years as needs dictated. The old wooden main buildings along Granite Street, the large four story brick dormitory that was located to the rear of the main buildings and the entire grounds were leveled in 1968 so that the new Cottages of Mount St. Ann could be built.

April 8, 1967 - Before Mount St. Ann is razed there was a Final Reunion of 200-300 former residents of St. Anne's Orphanage 133 Granite Street. Worcester's biggest family whose members were separated by thousands of miles and three generations returned to Mount St. Ann (formally St. Anne's Orphanage) on April 8 to visit the home of their memories before it was razed after 75 years of bringing "love and charity". A banquet and dance was held that evening at the Driftwood Restaurant in Shrewsbury, Mass.

August 1968 - The 25 children living at the home were moved to the former Newman House of the Roman Catholic Diocese of Worcester at 201 Salisbury Street. Most of the home's staff was moved to a smaller diocese owned building on Ward Street. The Ward Street building had served as headquarters for the local St. Vincent de Paul Society.

1968 - Demolition of the 1923 built, outmoded brick dormitory building was completed in the summer. Shortly afterwards the remaining buildings were torn down in preparation for five cottages (which could accommodate a total of 40 children) and an administration building, a one-story brick structure all costing $900,000.

Oct. 16, 1968 - Groundbreaking ceremony for the new Mount St. Ann administration building and five cottages. Two cottages were for boys ages 5-12, two for girls ages 5-12, and the last for girls ages 13-16. The administration building housed a chapel, kitchen facilities, auditorium, social worker offices, administration offices and quarters for the Sisters of Charity

April 13, 1970 - The Grey Nuns and their charges moved into the new Mount St. Ann cottages. The official dedication was held on May 1, 1970

February, 1979 - The Calkins Report on the Mount St. Ann Child Care Center stated; since 1970, nearly eight years, the nuns have had no additions or replacements and none are foreseen. Being stretched in all capacities, they feel they can no longer maintain a long term presence here.

April 3, 1979 - The Diocese of Worcester assumed ownership and took over operation.

Jan. 15, 1983 - Diocese Closes Mount St. Ann was closed for good. After serving 92 years as a refuge for orphans, underprivileged, neglected or abused children, the Granite Street home was ordered by its board of directors to shut down because of "underutilization," according to the Rev. Edmond T. Tinsley, director of Catholic Charities. Father Edmond said the home had recently provided emergency child care through the state Department of Social Services. Two of the cottages were housing residents in Catholic Charities' half-way program for alcoholics who formerly lived in Crosier House on Chrome Street. Another cottage housed a large Asian refugee family and yet another was occupied by a mother and her seven children. Also on the site was the office of the Diocesan Coalition for Peace and Justice.

1983 - Mount St. Ann becomes the **Christian Charities of Worcester Youville House**

The founder of the Grey Nuns of Montreal, Mother d'Youville was born on Oct. 15, 1701 in the Province of Quebec, Canada. In 1959 Marguerite d'Youville was beatified (the first step to sainthood) by Pope John XIII who called her the "Mother of Universal Charity". She was canonized in 1990 by Pope John Paul II. Her name is now prominent at the 133 Granite street site.

1987 - The Grey Nuns cleaned out their possessions from their rented three-decker apartment on Chrome Street and bid good-bye to Worcester.

2015 - As we visit the site at 133 Granite Street we get a feeling of sadness and loss for the place we used to call home. We may have lived there for a week, a month, a year or two, or even until we passed on to adulthood. It was our home. Now the playground and pool area belongs to a private child care pre-school facility. The buildings of Mount St. Ann are falling prey to the weather and neglect and are scheduled to be demolished. The Grotto across the street hasn't seen kindness in many a year. It appears that as we grow older and lose the beauty of our youth, so does the home of our youth. At least we can share our memories.

Please feel free to email us at St.AnnesOrphanage.Worcester@gmail.com with any correction and/or additions, pictures and/or memories to share. Thank you – The Family members of The French-Canadian Orphanage of Worcester, St. Anne's Orphanage, St. Ann's Orphanage, Mount St. Ann, and the Youville House.

Search for St. Ann's Orphanage Worcester on Facebook or the internet

About the Authors:

Rosalie Massie Blackburn
Rosie was a border at St. Anne's Orphanage between 1954-55. Her retirement after 19 years from the University of Florida's housing department coincided with her husband Rick's untimely passing in 2015. They shared 35 wonderful years together. He gave her the courage to follow her childhood dreams and memories. That led her to work side-by-side with her brother Joe, traveling in search of historical facts and browsing the internet for stories from past St. Anne's residents.

Joseph Massie
Joe was a border at St. Anne's Orphanage between 1954-55. Upon leaving the orphanage he and his sisters grew up with their mom and step-dad in Wollaston, MA (a part of Quincy) After graduating High School in 1968, he served four years in the United States Navy. He is now retired after 40 years in the computer field service industry. He and his wife Christine have been married for 44 years and live in Alachua, FL. Together, with his sister Rosalie, they coupled their efforts to publish The Ghosts of St. Ann's.

Made in the USA
Middletown, DE
28 March 2019